EVERYONE YOU HATE IS GOING TO DIE

EVERYONE YOU HATE IS GOING TO DIE

And Other Comforting Thoughts
on Family, Friends, Sex, Love, and
More Things That Ruin Your Life

Daniel Sloss

Alfred A. Knopf   New York   2021

Library of Congress Cataloging-in-Publication Data
Names: Sloss, Daniel, author.
Title: Everyone you hate is going to die : and other comforting
thoughts on family, friends, sex, love, and more things
that ruin your life / Daniel Sloss.
Description: New York : Alfred. A Knopf, 2021. |
Identifiers: LCCN 2020007979 (print) | LCCN 2020007980 (ebook) |
ISBN 9780525658146 (hardcover) | ISBN 9780525658153 (ebook)
Subjects: LCSH: Interpersonal relations—Humor.
Classification: LCC PN6231.I625 S56 2020 (print) |
LCC PN6231.I625 (ebook) | DDC 818./602—dc23
LC record available at https://lccn.loc.gov/2020007979
LC ebook record available at https://lccn.loc.gov/2020007980

Jacket image: tawatchai.m / Shutterstock
Jacket design by Keenan
Photograph of Daniel Sloss by Gavin Evans

Manufactured in the United States of America

First Edition

To my loving family—Lesley, Martyn,
Josie, and the two other ones

Contents

Contents

EVERYONE YOU HATE IS GOING TO DIE

Introduction

I Might Ruin Your Life, and You're Very Fucking Welcome

I'm thirty years old, and I have signed five separate divorce papers.

None of them were mine. Don't worry. I was merely autographing the papers of people whose divorces I've caused. They lined up, in the rain, to meet me and thank me for causing their breakup and then asked me to sign the papers as a memento of their lives—which they said I had saved. Like a white Jesus.

If that opening doesn't get you to buy this book, then honestly, just put it down and fuck off. It's not for you. I don't even want you to read it. Have a wonderful life.

Still here? Brilliant. Thanks for the money.

Now, I'd love to tell you that I had caused the divorces by giving these people the best sex of their lives. Fucking their brains out so good and proper that the only logical conclusion they could arrive at was to leave their subpar partners (not to be confused with sub partners—you kinky little shit) and beg me to spend the rest of my life with them. In fact, it's *my* book, I *will* tell you that. That's what happened. Really, my dick game is so good I caused divorces.

Okay, not really. It wasn't my dick game. It was my oral game. I *verbally* convinced these people to break up with their partners. I know, the dick thing is more believable. But this really is true. People watch my stand-up special *Jigsaw*—streaming worldwide on Netflix—and they decide they have to split with their partners. It's like The Ring, but for shitty relationships.

At this moment in time, the tally stands at more than 300 divorces, 350 canceled engagements, and more than 120,000 breakups.

"People watched a stand-up special and actually broke up with their life partners?" HAHAHAHAHAHA, I know! Right!? Unreal. And not humbling whatsoever. Any celebrity who says success is humbling is absolutely full of shit, by the way. I've been a Z-list celebrity for about twelve months now, and I feel like a fucking god. O. J. Simpson was a scumbag of a human being and what he did was horrific, but I now officially understand why he thought he could get away with it. If you're famous, people believe you. They think you're smart. They trust you. They buy your book. Fools.

For the past few years of my life, I've had a very untraditional view of love. Some would call it skeptical, pessimistic, and outright offensive. Some—me and at least 120,000 other people—would call it absolutely spot-on. I'll allow you to arrive at your own conclusions. Despite what Twitter will tell you, you and I are allowed to disagree on matters and still be cool. We cool? We cool.

When I was younger, I was obsessed with the idea of love and marriage. I wanted to have kids (still do) and be married by twenty-one (thank a nonexistent God I amn't). I was trying to emulate my parents. They met at nineteen, married at twenty-one, and by twenty-five were parents to a future comedian with a love of swearing and an ill-fitting God complex. My parents are in love. Still. To this day. After all these years. They are total nerds.

Oh, they argue and disagree, and I'll get texts from my mum letting me know my father is a big, rude idiot. And he, well, he just loves her, from what I can see. They bicker, they fight, but I also know for a fact that they fuck like teenagers and I reckon they're into some proper filth. Let's leave it at that. My gran might read this. (Though I also happen to have the same suspicions about that randy old tart. You can't have three kids without loving sex. Unless you're a devout Catholic. And even then I imagine knowing God is watching, like a cuck, makes it even sexier.)

I'm very aware that many parents do an excellent job of hiding their problems from their kids, keeping up the illusion of a happy marriage just long enough so that the kids get out to university and can deal with their own traumas there, far away, with other emerging alcoholics, druggies, and losers. Maybe my parents are incredible actors. Maybe they're holding out until my youngest brother goes to university next year. I doubt it. But only time will tell.

This relationship dynamic spans most of my entire family. Both sets of grandparents are not only alive—or they were at the start of writing this book (RIP Grandpa Sloss)—but also still in love with the eighty-year-old version of the twenty-year-old stunner they fell for. Only one separation in a huge family tree. With that example set from childhood, how the hell did I end up the first one not to be married before he turned twenty-five? The only one to show no sign of having kids before he's thirty? The only one that has had a threesome? Well, probably for the same reason I'm the first one in the family tree not to go to university. Because I'm a fucking idiot.

No. Kidding. It's because of a plethora of other reasons that I'll get into over the course of this book. Which is about relationships, by the way. Can't remember if I mentioned that. And not just about love. Relationships with everyone and everything. I'm nothing if not way too ambitious.

I used to believe in true love and "the One." But I also used to believe in Santa and Bitcoin. People change. All through school I was desperate to get a girlfriend. I didn't have a particular girl in mind. Anyone would have done. I just wanted a girlfriend. That's what people my age had, and girlfriends turned into wives and eventually mothers. Partners were glorified Pokémon, as far as I was concerned. I didn't need to catch them all. But I definitely needed one. I'd've taken a fucking Weedle at that point.

I fell in love every single year during my time at school. I mean, I obviously wasn't in love with them. But I didn't know that. I was a twat. A twat filled with new hormones and an impossibly high bar on love. A twat that just wanted to find that other half he'd seen everyone else find. A mimic twat. If you're reading this—Katherine, Sam, Laura, "other Laura," Christine, Karen, Nicola, Lynsey, Lisa, Danielle, Rachel, and Rhiannon—I now understand and forgive you for showing me absolutely zero interest. And thank you for putting up with my incredibly awkward displays of affection. (I made one of them a clay hedgehog pencil holder. The fucking state of me.)

None of that put me off, though. My "One" was out there and she definitely lived in the same country as me, so I'd work it out. That's what fate does, right? Throws your soul mate in front of you and goes, "Hey, dickhead, looking for this?"

Fate, being fate, answered my prayers. Either that or it saw me masturbating myself into a scab and decided not only to throw me a bone but to give the opportunity *to* bone.*

My first *real* girlfriend was great. I'll change her name, not because we didn't end well but just because I need a defense if she doesn't like how she's portrayed in this. I can try and claim it was a different first, real girlfriend. In this, we'll just call her Scarlett Johansson.

---

* Oh, you thought this was a highbrow book that's above that type of joke? Well, I was given creative freedom and was actively implored to speak in my true voice, so why don't you teabag a bollard?

(*Teabag* is a term for clunking your testicles in a sleeping or deceased person's mouth. A *bollard* is a post used to block cars from going on the sidewalk.)

I dated Scarlett Johansson for two and a half years. It was exactly as I'd imagined. We were in love, my parents loved her, her parents loved me. (All parents do. Seriously. You have no idea the level of charm I can pull out of my ass when I'm wooing partners' parents. I'm a godsend.) We holidayed together and we talked about our wedding and argued about kids and all that sort of mythical cultured shit you think being an adult actually entails. She was studying to be a lawyer. I was writing jokes about the length and width of my cock. It's a wonder we didn't work out.

Thing is, the comedy started going well. I got a few TV appearances, sold out my Edinburgh Festival run, and was even invited to Australia to do the festivals out there. Scarlett Johansson was one of the first girls ever to show me any interest. That's why I thought she was "the One"—because she was the only "One" nice enough to date me. But now I was suddenly confident. All those rejections from high school were a thing of the past. There was suddenly a new option that had never existed before—complete and utter sluttery.

I wanted to experience that single life I'd never had. You know, the single life where you have sex? That one. That might sound shallow, and that's because it was. So was I. I was twenty. I was in comedy. Everyone I knew had had mind-blowing amounts of sex in their lives. I wanted that. I idealized it.

That's what I think the actual number-one cause of divorce is—curiosity. People who got married too young or didn't sleep around enough in their youth suddenly thinking, *Wow, I bet being single would be great. I'd get to fuck loads and be my own person.* And they might be right. But they also might be wrong. I absolutely love being single. And not just because of the sex, but because, at this point in time, I have to think only about myself.

There is nothing wrong with being selfish as long as you're not selfish every second of every fucking day. Making decisions for the benefit of yourself should not be frowned upon unless it infringes upon the happiness of others. Using that one selfish moment to backstab all your workmates so you get a promotion and then firing them all to absorb their salary is, although baller, still wrong. You're directly screwing up people's lives for your own gain.

Deciding that you need time to work out who you are, what you want, and why is something that's best done by yourself. This might involve a breakup, and your making that decision will almost certainly make your partner sad, and that's definitely selfish. But here are two important things to remember:

One. You are not responsible for the happiness of other human beings. You are absolutely allowed to do everything within your power to make them happy, and you should. But it is not your fucking job. And if it feels like your job, quit. That's not a relationship. That's a job. Fuck that.

Two. Breakups suck. Always. No exceptions. Anyone who said they had a clean breakup is a self-centered psycho with no emotions who wasn't able to see the hurt in the other person. Even small inconsequential relationships coming to an end can have a huge effect on you, not just the person you're dumping, even if it's mutual. I've called things off with fuck buddies at times in our lives and there's always a part of me that goes, "Damn, that person is no longer in my life anymore." Just because everything wasn't right doesn't mean *some* things weren't right, so it's sad. It's a chapter ending.

Oh, and if you're reading that and saying, "But we can just stay friends!," fuck you, you absolute spanner. "We can stay friends" is like having a dog die and your parents telling you "You can still play with it."*

You can absolutely be friends with an ex of yours, but waaaaay later. When you break up with someone you cut every single part of them out of your life. Every. Single. Part. Photos, clothes, pets. Burn 'em all. Get off their fucking Netflix account. Delete them on all forms of social media. Text their mum to never text you again. Punch their gran. I don't care. Every form of them must be out of your life.

That might sound drastic, but it's important. Being in a relationship is a beautiful thing. Love is wonderful. Despite what people will tell you about me, I do not hate love. I hate fake love, and the problem is most of you morons can't tell the difference between real and fake because you're in a

---

* This is not my line, but rather a line used on me when I broke up with a girl and said, "We can still be friends." Thanks, and sorry again, Kirsty. You were right.

relationship. Just like I don't know when I'm in one. Love is a chemical imbalance in the brain that has more drastic side effects than drug addiction. You want me to cite evidence for that claim?* Just trust me and beware: Relationships can change you entirely. They almost always do.

You meet someone perfect and great and beautiful and they eat ass, but also your mum loves them, and oh, God, she just kissed your mum on her cheek with her ass-eating mouth, oh, no, your asshole and your mum are now only two degrees of separation and that degree of separation is now talking to Dad, oh, God, maybe Dad eats ass, it might be genetic, who knows, maybe you're one degree of separation from your mother's asshole. Oh, God.

(If you're wondering why I've put in so many rimming references, allow me to explain. I've never written a book before. I know there are editors and publishers who are going to read through this and give me notes. I'm just curious to see if there is ever a point where one of them emails me saying, "Fewer rimming references," because I'd frame that fucking email. Downside is maybe they don't care. Maybe they let it go through. Now it's a Mexican stand-off. I don't actually want all these references in there. It makes me look like a pervert. My gran's gonna read this. She can't know.)

I digress. You meet this great person who loves you, too.

* Cite my balls.

11

What an idiot! Look at this perfect moron hanging around with an absolute liability like yourself. So you want to be your best self because she's the best (or he is) and she or he is giving you the best so it's only fair. Unfortunately, you don't know how to be great, so you go to this amazing person and you let her/him lead you into becoming a better person.

Sometimes they nail it. And that's true love and those two nerds stay together, improving each other until one of them dies and the other never recovers emotionally, becomes a shell of her former self, forgets who she is, and rots to death in a nursing home. Too bleak? Phone your gran.

Other times, partners abuse this power. Manipulate it. Use your insecurity against you to make changes you may never recover from. Turn themselves into a deity-like figure from whom you constantly seek approval and validation because they've cut you off from the people who loved you before. I've been there and it's really not fun. More on that later—I just want to give you all something to look forward to.

Most of the time, though, you just change each other in little ways. You get them into comic books. They get you into hill-walking. At first by saying things like, "If we get to the top, I'll go down on you," but by the tenth time it's "Did you pack the sandwiches?" They don't like sports as much so you watch less of them, fully willingly of course. You want to spend more time with this person. But when you're no longer with this person, all that fucking free time and free personality become available again. You no longer have another half, so you actually now have another half to fill.

Now you can get back into football. Or you can stop climbing blowjob-less mountains. You can start a new hobby. You can eat meat again. You can drink more. You can drink less. You can reconnect with people your other half didn't have time for. But mostly you can just be you and do what you want to do, and you can keep the changes that they made that you like.

My relationship with Scarlett Johansson was great. I don't have a single bad word to say about her. She improved me as a human being. She made me happy. Made me confident. And then I was ready to use that happiness and confidence to leave her and go fuck random people like I'd always wanted to.*

That breakup sucked dick. And it was mutual as hell. A bit too mutual, if I'm being honest. She cried, but there wasn't much resistance. I said we should break up. She agreed. We both still cried for ages and it took me a solid twenty weeks/women to recover.

Don't let the fact that a breakup is going to suck stop you from going through with it. If you want evidence of why that is a bad idea, look at your unhappily married friends and family. I guarantee you they missed the breakup window years ago. Acknowledge the fact that the breakup is going to suck, go through with it, rip that person's entire

* She's now happily married to a much better man, so fuck your pseudo-empathy.

13

world from beneath his feet, watch him crumble, and then go buy yourself a well-earned milkshake and get back in the fucking game.

It's waaaaay crueler to *not* dump that person. If you happen to be in a relationship with someone you don't want to be with, allow me to try and inspire you to get out of it.

If you persist in having relationships that have no future and you don't dump them, you are a fucking monster. A selfish, cowardly, pathetic monster. Every second you are with them you are taking something valuable away from them and hurting their recovery. There is no future in this. You know this, they don't. How dare you string them along, make them feel safe, and waste that valuable time that they could use to find someone with a better dick/pussy than you. Someone who actually likes them, unlike you, you coldhearted dead-behind-the-eyes witch.

Hope that helped.

Side note: Never, ever allow someone else to become your other half. Jesus fucking Christ. Have some self-respect. You're a full-grown biological, statistical anomaly that has cognitive thought standing on a rock that's hurtling through an infinite universe, could you stop being so fucking basic, please? You are you. They are them. Together you are a couple. If your other half completes you, why on earth didn't you try to fill that void yourself first? Don't answer. I'll tell you. It's because you're a fucking twat.

I should point out that this book is going to involve a lot of swearing. Not as much as I had originally wanted—

that's editors for you—but still enough to hurt your delicate American sensibilities. Allow me to explain. I come from a magical part of the world where swearing doesn't matter too much. It's called "Bonnie Scotland," and despite our vast reserves of oil, you have yet to invade it. Thanks, guys.

I understand if you don't know a lot about us. England has pretended we don't exist in every election that has ever taken place. We're weird by your standards and you're off-the-wall insane by ours. If you buy a laptop in Scotland there is no space bar on the keyboard. It's just the word *fucking.* Despite what some people say, I do find swearing to be both "big" and "clever." My gran always said "Swearing shows a lack of vocabulary." Does it, bitch tits? As far as I can see, I use at least ten more words than you.

I understand that I swear too much. I get that. Swearing is different where I'm from. *Cunt* is only an insult some of the time. In Scotland you can be a "good cunt" or a "bad cunt," but your status as "cunt" is not up for negotiation. My mother calls me that word. Sometimes I forget that it's a word that offends people because I'm normally surrounded by adults who don't get upset at specific noises (although my American editor keeps cutting it out of this book, the cunt).

Imagine if other words caused the same visceral reaction from people. You and I are having a lovely conversation in a café. You casually mention the word *yogurt* in an anecdote and I stop you, mid-sentence, saying I find your use of that word "pathetic." I'm genuinely upset by your use of the word *yogurt*. I've never said "yogurt." Not even when I stub my toe. How could you possibly say that? There are children here. Children who now, thanks to me, know a word that gets a reaction. A word that has power because I gave it power. Deep down, the only reason I hate the word *yogurt* is because I know that everyone calls me a "whiny little yogurt" behind my back.

People that are offended by swearing are the most pathetic breed of human being that has ever stepped foot on this planet. I can't even call them children. Because children don't give a shit about swearing. But these people can have their entire day ruined by the use of a word. The uttering of a single syllable can cause these fuckwits to lose their minds, to write letters of complaint. TO OTHER ADULTS!

If I can offend you by swearing, imagine how much I could hurt you if I actually tried. Jesus titty-fucking Christ. I can't imagine allowing a person to have that much control over me. Hating a word so much that upon hearing it I lash out and become genuinely emotional. Believing that the fact that you even used that word negates every good point you made. People who think like this are not worthy of our attention. They are only worthy of our disdain. So if you fall into that category, I have two things to say to you. One: Well done for making it this far in the book. Two: Fuck off, cunt.

After my relationship with Scarlett Johansson I was single for a very long time. I dabbled, occasionally dipping my toes into the water of relationships. Only to realize I probably didn't have the skills to survive in them if they were of any meaningful depth. Then after several years of fun I had one relationship that nearly ruined my life until it became the inspiration for my *Jigsaw* show. I've enjoyed being single. And a lot of being single involves looking at people in relationships and, through being outside the cloud of love, realizing what utterly stupid fucking morons most of them are.

The arrogance of people in relationships has always annoyed me. Especially when they rub that society-forced neediness down my throat as if I'm the one having a shit time because I didn't settle for the ninth best thing in my high school. Full offense to everyone who does this, by the way. Happiness should be something that fills you and completes you. Not something to boast about on Instagram or Facebook.

Telling random single people how happy you are in your relationship is like running up to a homeless person and showing them a wad of cash. At least that's what you think it's like because you're an idiot. A lot of the time, what you're actually holding is Monopoly money. You're running around the streets of the Internet showing everyone what a fat wad of cash you have and the rest of us are looking, going, "Don't they realize what they have is entirely fucking worthless?"

But, seeing as you decided to make happiness a competition, allow me to fucking win.

If you're one of these knobs who spends your entire online presence and social life constantly talking about how great your relationship is in front of your friends who aren't in relationships, I want you to know this. I want you to know that I know you're not happy. How do I know? Because I'm happy. And very rarely does the stuff I'm happy about make its way online because I am experiencing it then and there. I don't talk about how great my friends are online because I tell them to their face. I don't brag about how well my career is going because I understand that I got my career with a fair bit of luck and a lot of others weren't afforded the same opportunities I was. I just enjoy my job and try to keep it going. The reason you are typing out how much you love your partner isn't to convince the world you love them. You are trying to convince yourself. And I see right fucking through you.

Normally, if you are happy for a reason that I find stupid, like you think there is a heaven or that your baby is cute, I would let it go. As long as you're happy and not hurting anyone, who cares? But you *are* hurting people. By giving in to this societal conditioning that tells us we all must be with someone no matter the cost, you are lying about the benefits of settling to everyone around you, saying that being in a shit relationship is better than being alone. Somebody who has been alone for a while, struggling with it as we all sometimes do, will now come across your performance piece on Facebook and think, *Fuck! Jenna is happy and her boyfriend is a giant fucking asshole. But look how happy she is!*

Even though he is literally the least interesting person on this entire planet, Jenna is still happy! Damn, maybe I should just do what Jenna did and try and polish whatever turd walks by me next. It must be better than being just me.

I'm not trying to discredit all relationships. I am surrounded by people who have found partners who love them, complement their personality, inspire each other, and laugh with them. That is what we should all strive to achieve. But if you can't find that, the next step is not "Well, I'll find someone who has one of those qualities." It's wait until the love of your life shows up.

It would be like saying, "Everyone else has a cake, but I only have flour. Well, no time to be picky. I might as well just spoon self-rising flour down my throat to see if that fills me up."

"How do I know if it's true love?" Simple. Is your reaction "Oh, my God. She's so perfect. I love her. I've never felt like this before. I can't go on without this person. I'm so happy I'm in love"? Congratulations! You're not in love. You're in love with the idea of love. You're in lust and I'm gonna laugh at you when this fails. And it will.

I believe love should be the most inconvenient thing in the world. Falling in love should be like, "Are you fucking kidding me? Shit. I was having a swell old time alone, and then this perfect dumbass turned up and now I want to be with her. What an absolute selfish prick this person is to come out of nowhere and make me feel this. Goddamn it. I was having fun. Oh, well."

My father explained it best, I think. My father always said he would die for us, his family. But he was never happy when he said it. He was never bragging. It wasn't a boast of his macho-ness. It was an inconvenient fact. I'm a dumbass who smokes too much weed and writes books criticizing relationships about which I have no inside knowledge. In the apocalypse, we'll need brilliant men like my father to rebuild the world, not men like me. But he'd still die for me. That's what love is. Utterly illogical. My dad would die for his family. He doesn't want to. But he would if necessary. Because he can't imagine a life without us.

I fully expect a bunch of you nerds in relationships to get upset by my views on this. That's fine. When I tell you my views on other types of relationships, I'm sure a bunch of other nerds will get upset. None of this is based in fact or peer-reviewed studies. They're just the conclusions I've drawn from my own unique experiences, and I'm applying them to your entirely different wealth of experiences. If you think I'm just some bitter single person trying to shit on everyone's parade, you're not entirely wrong.

I recommend enjoying this book with a beer/glass of wine/spliff, and a huge pinch of salt. I'm a comedian and my main goal is to make you laugh. I want you to snort out loud on a bus while reading this. I want you to read a line, then run over to your partner and go, "Oh, my God, he's absolutely nailed Abbie and David in this book! We should get them to read it. Hopefully it'll break them up."

I'm going to say a lot of things I don't mean, and I'm

going to mean a lot of things I don't say. If something winds you up, it's safe to assume that I meant it as a joke. Unless I specifically state otherwise. If said joke wasn't for you—fair. This book wasn't written just for you. I'm just trying to add a little bit of laughter to your day.

If I can make you think as well—brilliant. If I can make you get out of a shitty relationship—even better. But if I upset you? That's the pinnacle, baby. Your emotions are my Everest. Thank you for letting me conquer them. I'll stick a flag in your rage and let the world know I inspired genuine anger in a person I haven't even met. Eggplant emoji, splash emoji, splash emoji, splash emoji.

If you tell me the world is flat, I won't get mad at you and shout, because I know you're a fucking moron. My confidence in the fact that the world is round is so strong that whatever bullshit you try and throw at me isn't going to make me waver. Your point doesn't sway me, because I know you're an idiot. But I suspect my opinions do sway you. Some part of them hit home, and that doubt makes you angry because you haven't doubted any of that before. Or at least admitted that doubt. Who am I to do that? I'll tell you. I'm the fucking comedian who broke up 120,000 couples, caused 350 weddings to be canceled weeks before they happened, and is now being cited in divorce cases as one of the main causes.

Enjoy the fucking book.

Chapter 1

The Good, the Bad, and
the Totally Fucked-up

My mother has a Ph.D. in microbiology, is one of the leading experts in the world on global warming, and spends half her year in UN meetings, calling delegates from every corner of the planet "fucking morons" in a way that they're not really sure if they're being called "fucking morons" or not. They are. Both being called "fucking morons" and, I'm assured by Dr. Sloss, inhabiting the description.

To call my father a computer programmer is to do him a disservice. He's one of the smartest people on the planet (including you, Mum). I don't know what he studied or even what he does. All I know is he's a nerd. A serious one. If he hadn't raised me to be such a loving and caring and selfless and humble human being (with a huge cock), I'd beat him up for his lunch money every morning before he goes to work. He's been on *Robot Wars** multiple times, he's done animatronics for *Teenage Mutant Ninja Turtles,* and I

---

* The British version of *BattleBots.*

swear to God I once saw the man fix a refrigerator with a fucking hairdryer.

My mother is one of the kindest human beings I know. Apart from her breasts,* she's all heart. Christmas at my house has always been something out of a clichéd American holiday movie. A huge family sitting around a massive table piled high with food while the grandparents pull Christmas crackers† with the kids. My father talks to one of our neighbors who doesn't have anyone to spend Christmas with. I do shots with my underage brothers and my friends who have nowhere else to go and so become our family for the day. My mum wants everyone to feel included. She'd much rather have a well-earned glass of wine and hear about your day than argue over something we're both never going to agree on. She hardly ever raises her voice. But if she does, you're fucked.

---

* I have been mercilessly bullied about the size of my mother's breasts since high school. It's no secret that she is top-heavy. The only thing worse than being bullied about the size of your mother's breasts is the look of smug pride and satisfaction on your father's face when you tell him why you're being bullied.

† Oh, my fucking God, my American editor just told me no one in your backward country knows what pulling Christmas crackers means. They are a staple of British Christmases, as Christmasy as Christmas trees and Santa. A Christmas cracker is basically a small tube wrapped in Christmas wrapping paper, and inside is a cheesy paper hat; a cheap, shitty toy; and the worst fucking joke you have ever heard in your entire life. They are set around the table at every single place setting for Christmas dinner. You pull it with the person sitting next to you. Whoever gets the larger end (like a wishbone) wins the hot, crunchy prize (we're talking bottle openers and stupid stickers) and has to read the horrible joke out loud. I can't believe you don't have this. What a bunch of losers.

My father is a logical man. A reasonable man. A man of facts. He loves an argument because he is right and you are wrong. And 99 percent of the time that is true. Facts are facts, and opinions based on anything other than facts might as well be based in horseshit. Your emotions do not change statistics. Your gut feeling doesn't mean shit compared to peer-reviewed studies. Even your experiences don't really matter when compared to the median. He also taught me the finest lesson on arguing, and I now apply that to my stand-up every day: In an argument, you don't have to be right, you just have to convince the other person that they're wrong. That's a solid win. This isn't to say my father isn't a sweetheart. He is gentle, caring, and has never raised his hands to another person in his life. The pussy.

The combined swirling mess of DNA from these two created me. The force of their wildly different personalities raising me since my birth has created a constant war in my head between my insane desire not only to be right but also to make you fully aware of how wrong you are, battling with my, quite frankly, unfair levels of empathy for those who are wrong and who have fucked things up due to their wrongheadedness. This makes for an interesting and constant inner monologue.

I'm not complaining about my parents at all. I love them both dearly. I'm one of those losers who considers his parents among his friends. Unless I was being a piece of shit (which I often was as a teenager), they didn't treat me like a child. They treated me like a human being. Don't get me wrong, I wasn't an equal, they're not psychos. But I was definitely above indentured servant. Which is nice.

My mother is, purely and simply, one of the kindest human beings that walks this Earth. If everyone in the world was like my mother, there would be no war and I'd be a sad, sad virgin. She is a phenomenal woman, important to the health of the world, and, in her spare time, happens to be the best mother I could have asked for.

Like a lot of men, I think my father is one of the greatest men that has ever lived. To his very core he is a good human being. I am not even a tenth of the man my father is. When I'm a dad if I can even do half as good a job as my dad has done, then I'll have overachieved (once again).

I have a strong relationship with my parents. That's helped shape who I am over the years. Our parents are the first people we develop a substantial relationship with, and how that pans out has an impact on us for the rest of our lives.

It's why I find other people's parents fascinating. I love to meet my mates' parents just so I can try and work out what led to the car crash of a person I've chosen as a lifelong friend. Even better is meeting your partner's parents. What two creatures made and then programmed this thing that I can't seem to stop thinking about?

Some parents do such incredible jobs that you look at their child and see the perfect amalgamation of both parents fused into one kind, caring, and sensitive human being. Some parents do a total shit job, but miraculously they somehow create that same type of caring human being. Instead of having two parents who teach you right and wrong through positive examples, people arrive at the same point by fighting to be the opposite of their life-givers.

I fall into a different category, I think. I'm a decent human being, but I don't hold a candle to my parents. Especially intelligence-wise. They're geniuses. I am not. This isn't to say I think I'm a dumbass. My parents were too good and supportive for that. Part of me reckons that if I went on a murder spree for several years, despite their obvious disappointment, my dad would be impressed that I'd gotten away with it for so long and my mother would be proud that there was some sort of ethical code to my blood-filled rampage. "He killed twenty men and twenty women, and I think that's actually quite progressive. Please respect our family's privacy at this time."

Some parents do such poor jobs that they create children who are utterly detrimental to the human race. Every person who set the world back a couple of years had parents who were shit at what they did. I think it's weird that we just let anyone have kids. That's madness. Anyone? Have you met people?

If you want to drive a car, you have to be taught how to drive a car. You have to pass a test to be able to drive without supervision. You need to be insured so that if your car injures or kills someone, they or their loved ones can get compensation for your inability to drive properly. If you are a consistently terrible driver, at some point you will never be allowed to drive again, or at least you'll have your car taken away from you for a long enough time that you can improve your driving skills. But Alex Jones is just allowed to have kids when he wants to? Fuck that.

There should be qualifications to have kids. Some form of test that we all go through in order to prove that we're capable of raising another human being to the point where when they fuck it all up it's their fault, not ours. What's my plan for all of this? I'm glad you asked. Welcome to the plan I came up with that my mother called "a bit Hitler-y."

In the UK, at the age of thirteen, every pupil is brought to the assembly hall to be told that we're all going to get our inoculations against tuberculosis, because unlike Americans, we really don't like to spread diseases that were eradicated years ago. We don't have a hipster attitude about the plague. We tend to value the opinion of medical professionals over celebrities. Each to his or her own, I guess. America is the only country in the world where they'll give an actual, real-life, degree-having doctor the same amount of airtime as someone who believes in God for a living.

They think this is a balanced perspective: letting both sides of the argument be heard. It's not. If I were to get diagnosed with cancer in the UK, they'll only recommend a doctor to me. For, like, no money, too. They'll be, "Oh, that's a shit thing that happened to you. Let's bloody sort that out, shall we?" As opposed to the American, arcade-machine form of health care, which is "Please insert $100,000 to keep playing the game called life."

So the UK will get me a doctor who will say something doctor-y, along the lines of "There's heaps of cancer up in them balls, mate. Too much cancer for my liking. I'd recommend getting one of them bad boys lopped off, then we'll fill you with this medicine and let that cancer know who is really boss. Put your wallet away, life should be free. We're all humans."

Sometimes they'll offer a second opinion. But the weird thing is, they get the second opinion from another doctor. This one will say, "Deborah said you had to get your ball cut off? That's brutal. Typical Deborah. She's never had balls. She doesn't know the joy. I respectfully disagree. Balls are great. I reckon you can keep both. I think we should fill you with this type of medicine and it'll get rid of that cancer slower, but you'll still have both nuts by the end. Hitler had only one ball and look what happened to him. Vegetarian. Not worth the risk."

That, to us, is a balanced choice. Two professionals giving you two separate options, but toward the same goals. Americans think that's biased. Two doctors? That hardly seems fair. They both believe in medicine. Where's the idiot who believes in shoving crystals up your arsehole to get rid of the inside demons? Why is there not a man who wears a dress* letting us know that you can wish the cancer away? Just like Steve Jobs did.

Before you whiny Apple dweebs ping in your "Sent from my iPhone" emails with all sorts of complaints that I'm not going to read, Steve Jobs had pancreatic cancer and was given an 80 percent chance of survival if he did chemo right away. He decided not to. He decided to go vegan and sing to almonds or whatever fucking voodoo someone from L.A. made up instead of developing an actual useful skill. Weirdly enough, not treating pancreatic cancer leads to having loads more cancer. Who knew?† By the time he agreed medicine would work, it had gone down to a 20 percent chance of survival.

Then he died.

Good.

Stupid twat.

If you want to use alternative medicine, be prepared for the alternative results—being a dead idiot.

Anyway, in Scotland you get vaccinated whether you like it or not because it's widely agreed that doctors know more than Jenny McCarthy. So you all go down to the assembly hall, and they force everyone to get the shots. They then give you a big lecture on how the vaccination will work. It'll hurt, but then the wound will scab over. They'll repeatedly tell you how important it is to let this wound heal natu-

---

* And not in the sexy, cool way like us Scots do.
† Science. Science and Doctors knew.

rally, not to get it wet, and especially DO NOT PICK OR TOUCH THE SCAB, OTHERWISE IT WILL SCAR.

Then you spend the next week getting punched in the scab by every senior pupil. You walk down the corridor, and strangers will just punch you right in the vaccination. That's what their seniors did to them, and it's what you'll do to the freshmen next year. The circle of life.

If you look at the left shoulder of any British person born after the 1960s and before 2001 (when the shot changed), you will see a small circular scar. I have one. My mum has one. My dad has one. Everyone I know has one. This exists because ever since we were all told not to punch one another in the vaccination, we all punched one another in the vaccination because, deep down, everyone is an asshole.

What does this have to do with parenting? I'm getting there, calm down. My point is that this organization of everyone getting inoculated works. It has worked for years. There's no tuberculosis in the UK. We've done it. So I think we should use this system in other ways.

Did you know vasectomies are reversible? They're not permanent. You can undo them. You can also freeze sperm and save it for later (for baby having, not a quick popsicle). What I'm suggesting is at the age of thirteen, you get every boy in the UK into their school assembly hall, you give them a private room and a whole computer of porn, and you let nature take its course. You then have them collect their mess in a cup, stick their name on it, and then you give the little tyke a vasectomy. After the vasectomy you give them a bunch of ice cream and send them home to recover, and the girls can spend the rest of the day actually learning for once.

That way you can't make a baby by mistake. It can't be done. You should still totally wear a condom because of all the diseases they help prevent, but even if it tears you can't accidentally create human consciousness.

Let's say you get older and you're in a relationship and you decide that what your life is missing is a baby. You want to bring a child onto the planet. Cool. Good for you. All you have to do is apply to get your sperm back.

Now, this can't be a government-based thing. We can't have their evil standards of who would be a good parent and who wouldn't. It's got to be like jury duty. You get a letter in the mail saying, "Next week you have to come in to decide who gets a cup of their jizz back"—I'm paraphrasing, obviously. You and a panel of your peers, other regular people from society, look over applications from people who want to have kids. And here's the thing: Most of them will be allowed to have them.

Most of us aren't intentionally cruel. We're not going to base it on a couple's income, political beliefs, or looks. We're going to base it on how much they want kids. "Me and my girlfriend have been together for two years. It's been a short period of time, but from the bottom of my heart I can say that I have never loved someone more. We think we're ready to bring a child into this world. I'm a janitor and she's a barista, but we think we'd make good parents."

You and your peers ask a few important questions. "How many do you want to have? Three? That's a fine amount. Are you going to hit them? No? You promise? Good. Do you have any pets? Those seem trained, that's a good start. Sure. Congratulations." Done. Five-minute interview and the lady is on a bed, legs in stirrups, getting a turkey baster rammed up her vaginal cavity or whatever science is involved at that point. I'm not a doctor. Clearly.

Will this prevent bad people from being made? Of course not. But it'll certainly reduce it. No person that applies for kids is ever told "Never," just, "Not yet." You can give them a puppy for a year, see how the dog turns out. If they can't train a dog, they can't raise a human. That's basic maths.* You can even try and catch them out with small yet crucial questions.

"Would you force religion upon the child?"

"No, but as a Christian I would raise it with Christian values. We would explain why we believe in God and respect the child's decision either way."

"Great. Would you still accept the child if it was gay?"

"Of course. That's our child and we'll love it no matter what. As Republicans, we believe God made all humans, so to hold that against the child would be un-Christian and cruel."

"Amazing. Last question. What name would you call it?"

"Topher."

---

* *Maths* is fucking plural and I'll fight every last one of you eagle-shagging freedom fuckers.

"I'm so sorry, try again next year."

I'd go through the application process, too. And much like my actual driving test, I'd be allowed to have my sperm back after my third attempt. I'm still a bit immature and I'm also the man that came up with a plan that is eugenics-light, at best. So maybe I'm not going to be the best father. I'll respect that decision, should it be made.

I also probably wouldn't have been born had this existed when my parents had me. As I will explain in another chapter, I was an accident. Under the Sloss Sperm-Saving Program, my parents couldn't have accidentally conceived me, and thus I never would have been around to come up with this world-saving concept.

There is literally no flaw in any of this plan. No further questions.

That's the weird angle all those anti-abortion ads go for. I don't know if you've seen them, but they're essentially a picture of a lady or a man with the quote, "Steve invented the cure for racism. But, unfortunately, he was aborted to death and didn't do that. Abortion—just say No" or some shit like that. Their point that "by having an abortion you've eliminated the guy who would have cured racism and we could really do with him right now. Nice one, slut" is an interesting angle and one that I think pro-choice people should adopt. Just put a picture of Martin Shkreli, that little pharma-bro cunt, with the words "Abortion— once you pop you just can't stop." I always find it weird that pro-life states are also the states that are pro–death penalty.

It's almost as if there's no logic to it and they learned their ethics from a two-thousand-year-old pocket book of psalms peddled by pathetic pedophiles preaching to petulant preschool-educated pricks. God, I love alliteration. And I hate God.

Not only am I pro-choice, I'm anti-parent. There are some people who just should not be parents, end of fucking story. They suck, they're bad people, they have no desire to improve, and they're going to pass these traits on to others.

I don't think you should be allowed to hit kids, but I do think I should be allowed to hit you if your kid is being really annoying. Some people don't take enough responsibility for their children. My mum and dad never hit me, but they never made me anyone else's problem. If I was being a shit in public, I was immediately taken away from the public and punished until I decided to not be such a little twat.

Some parents will just inflict their shit kids on the world. They'll take their non-toilet-trained puppy to a carpet store and ruin everyone else's shopping trip. I think I'm well within my rights to smack you across the back of your negligent little head and go, "Hey, sort that the fuck out. Train it. I know you don't want to be inside with it all day, but you made that choice when you decided being a parent was a part-time endeavor."

I'm not claiming raising a kid is easy, but it's also nowhere near as hard as some parents make it look. I think my parents did a pretty good job. Some of you will disagree, I'm sure. But don't forget that I already have your money. So whose parents were dumber?

I've seen people I fundamentally disagree with on most points turn out to be incredible mothers and fathers. I came from a working-class area of Scotland where some of my peers had kids at sixteen or even younger. I judged them at the time. Of course I did. I thought I was better than them. Out of morbid curiosity and schadenfreude, I stayed friends with them on Facebook. I wanted to see how they fucked up their lives as well as their kids' lives.

I've never been happier to be wrong. These people who I thought were scum of the earth, dumb little fucking chavs with no future, absolutely stepped up to bat. They produced happy kids, smart kids, kind kids, beautiful kids. Kids that wouldn't judge other kids, like I did. Most of the people you hate in this world love the ever-loving fuck out of their children, and, despite your protests, that makes them profoundly human.

The only difference between me and these people that I wrongly judged is that one day I'll probably have to go fully back on my word and ask their twenty-year-old kids to babysit for my four-year-old. And they'll nail it. The job, that is.

I'm desperate to be a dad. Before I knew I wanted to be a comedian, I knew I wanted to be a dad. I love kids. I have two younger siblings and several younger cousins. A dead sibling, too. Little makes you appreciate children more than seeing one go too soon. That potential just . . . gone.

I've been raised around babies. Even the ugly babies are brilliant. And yes, there are ugly babies, this isn't Disney. Let's be real. Some of them are disgusting, chubby little rotters. But they're still brilliant. There is a comedian in the UK who I love dearly, who has the ugliest kid I have ever seen in my life. Oh, my God. This child is absolute pedo-proof. You could punt this thing over the fence into the garden of a sex offenders' unit and it would only come back with a tan and a warden holding the young'un as far away as possible so he wouldn't have to look it in the face.

That being said, it's still a great kid. The parents don't know it's ugly. They truly don't. They'll read this book and think it's about someone else's child. That's the power of parental love. That's what I want. My kids might be hideous little fucks, but I'll never know. They'll look like me, and as a narcissist I'll just think, *There it goes, the most beautiful child that ever lived. Pasty white with a huge penis. That's my girl.*

I can't help myself around babies. I need to squeeze them. Not to death, but almost. You know when a baby is crying and you have to distract it by jangling keys? Babies are my keys. If I'm crying, hand me a baby and I'll be happy. Or at least I'll have found someone who is happy to cry with me. I get it from my father. If my mum would let him, my dad would have another five kids.

In all honesty, as much as I respect people who don't want to have kids, I think you're fucking pointless. Why are you here? The only reason any form of life exists is to reproduce. If it doesn't, it isn't life. Base-level science. Pandas are an abomination.

If you don't want kids, I absolutely get it. There are enough people on this dying planet. There are, at best, fifty years of life left on Earth. You don't want to bring a child into that? Well done, you. Smart. Ethical. Forward-thinking. I don't mind you lot. I disagree with your reasoning, but I understand your conclusions. I'm still going to bring kids into this world, because even when I do eventually have to kill them to save them from the burden of living on a planet with unbreathable air and a lack of water, at least I'll have done what I was put on this planet to do.

Those of you that hate kids? Broken humans. Spare parts. To not want kids is absolutely fine. The world is fine without any more children. You saw a loophole, you took it, I respect that. You're playing free-roam on Grand Theft Auto with all the weapons but having played none of the game. You see a kid, you think *Cute,* you hold it, you like it, you give it back, you still don't want one. Cool. You and I are different, but I respect your beliefs and thank you for holding my child. But if you actively hate all children, I am thrilled that your legacy, and your broken DNA, dies with you.

I'm not even sure I fully believe that opinion. I just

got a little bit of wind in my sails once I realized all my childless friends would get angry and upset about it and I'll inevitably win because they'll die and they won't have a new generation to defend their dumb shitty opinion. History is written by my wiener.

Chapter 2

Siblings: How to Deal with Them and How to Profit Off of Dead Ones

I have a dead sister. My sister is dead. I once had a sister, she is dead now. Death, one. Sister, nil. Knock, knock. Who's there? Not my sister. And so on and so forth. I still haven't found the best way to convey that little nugget of information to others, although I'm pretty sure I've found the funniest.

Josie was great. She was the best person I ever knew. She had full-blown cerebral palsy. That's not the official diagnosis. The official diagnosis from the doctor to my mother was "Your daughter is a spastic."

You see, the word *spastic* wasn't offensive until a bunch of pricks heard the word *spastic* and started calling people who weren't spastics "spastics," and now we all get very uncomfortable around that word. I say "we," but I really mean you lot. I have no problem using the word, seeing as it's a fucking medical term and my intent is to convey information, not hatred.

I do hate when the "retard" debate comes up, and I'm

not talking about Brexit. Some asshole says the word *retard* to describe someone we all can't stand and suddenly there is a huge debate about the use of the word as opposed to people agreeing that the "victim" of the word is in fact a fucking moron. People will then talk and debate about how offensive the word is and how it's used to demean people.

Any word can be made offensive if yelled with enough vitriol and spite from a moving van. Look at the word *snowflake,* for fuck sake. That's now an insult. Can we please all agree that apart from a select few words (the *N-word* and *faggot,* both of which are steeped in barbaric history, and the etymology of both are incredibly cruel), no words are actually offensive in themselves? The intent behind their use is.

When you use the word *retard,* I don't think of Josie. I don't associate that word with disability at all. To me a retard is a person who is thick as pig shit, like Gwyneth Paltrow. Josie wasn't stupid. She couldn't walk or talk, but I'll tell you right now she had sass. You don't need control of your leg muscles to roll your eyes.

I have never used that word to describe a person with disabilities. Unless, of course, they say something profoundly stupid, like, "I identify as a penguin." I also won't use that word in public dialogue or onstage. Even though the word doesn't offend *me,* I understand other people have a different history with the word. I can't change their experiences. Nor will I deny them it. I wouldn't want to encourage people to use the word publicly because I can't guarantee they don't mean it. I'll just use the word privately, like most of us do anyway.

It's only in later life I realized that Josie wasn't a "normal" sibling. Now that I've seen and experienced different sibling relationships, I understand that perhaps what I had wasn't run-of-the-mill. But it was fun. If you've never had a disabled sibling or relative, then my heart sincerely goes out to you. It's a fucking joy.

It's been twenty-two years since Josie died, and I can still hear her laugh. That laugh lit up the world. Nothing since then has ever compared to it. My future psychiatrist will probably be able to draw a connection between Josie's laugh and my dream of becoming a comedian. I would struggle to disagree with them. My whole family would try to make Josie laugh as often as we could because it was the sound of unfiltered happiness.

Having a disabled sibling can be difficult at points, but not all the time. All the other siblings of disabled people are going to hate me for telling the rest of you muggles about the many, many advantages of having a disabled family member. But we've had it too good for too long, so here we go.

The parking is unreal. You get to park insanely close to the place you need to be, despite the fact that the disabled person is in a wheelchair. Josie's legs were never tired. She could have been parked a mile away and it would have made no difference to her life whatsoever. But you can go fuck yourself if you think we were ever going to point that out.

With the parking, though, comes the judgment. If you

park in a disabled parking space, you get to witness people assessing whether you are disabled *enough* to deserve that space. Because they're jealous, as they should be. They stand there watching you leave the vehicle, sincerely hoping to see a limp or a slaver.*

My parents and I have always hated these people. Disability is not always visible. Don't get me wrong; Josie's disability was incredibly visible. You could see it from space. Nobody is that happy every second of every day without something being wrong with them mentally. But we liked to fuck with the judgers. So if we ever saw someone staring at us as we parked, we made sure to bring out Josie last. Dad would get out first. Absolutely fine. Bit of a belly on him, but not enough for a mobility scooter by a long shot. Then Mum would get out. Nothing wrong with her except for the man that she married. Then I'd get out, completely fine. Only thing wrong with me was the bowl cut my parents forced me to have until I was ten.

At this point the judgers would be furious. An entire family of fully abled people parking in the parking space of those less fortunate. How very dare we? AND THEN THE UNVEILING. Dad opens up the side door of the Toyota Previa (please sponsor this book, Toyota. We sincerely loved that car. Perfect for a family with a spastic. There's your

---

* Scottish word for spittle coming out the side of your mouth. Pronounced SLAY-VERR, with the hardest R you've ever rolled in your whisky-less life. For the more keen-eyed Yanks out there, you'll notice there isn't an "e" in whisky. That's because there isn't. Consider this revenge for taking the "u" out of colour.

new slogan. Thank me later. Pay me now) and we bring out Grand Madam herself. Shit-eating grin and more often than not a shit-filled diaper. Scooped ungracefully out of the car and plopped into the wheelchair, laughing every second of the kerfuffle.

The guilt that crossed these people's faces will fuel me until the day I die. My parents and I would laugh and laugh and naturally Josie would join in, as that was her favorite thing to do, and we would go about the rest of our lives.

The second advantage to having a cripple/spazz/mong/ whatever-word-you-use-to-demean-people-who-have-a-larger-capacity-for-love-than-you as a family member is theme parks. Oh, my fucking God. There are an infinite number of things I miss about Josie, but right up there is taking her to theme parks.

First off, straight to the front of every single line. Without fail. As a seven-year-old I suddenly learned that my sister was a golden ticket to every theme park. They treated her like royalty. Not only would we get to the front of the line, but Josie's laugh was so infectious that by the time we made it back to the start of the ride they would just let us go around again and again and again and again.

Have you ever been in an ambulance going ninety miles an hour at the age of seven and the driver lets you put on the sirens? No. You haven't. Hahaha. Suck my dick. I have. It's so cool. Sure, Josie was having a seizure, but she always did. That was her thing. That and fits and every other health issue and inconvenience that come with disabilities.

None of that might sound normal. But it was. And it is. Maybe not to you, but you don't get to tell the world what normal is, especially with your Pornhub search history. If you talk to my parents about Josie, they might tell you a different version of our childhoods. One with uncertainty and struggles. I doubt it, though. They loved her the same way I did.

Josie went to a different school from mine. What with me being a genius and her being literally retarded, it was only fair. But there were days where she came into my school, too. I can't remember why. I'm sure for the other kids it was a lesson in tolerance and understanding. But for me it was my baby sister coming into school. I loved showing her off. She wasn't like Craig's younger brother, who was annoying and cried all the time. She wasn't like Lisa's younger sister, who stole all her toys. My sister was the happiest person alive *and* she was in a cool-as-fuck robot chair.

I remember being protective over her. I think that's one of the first lessons you learn as a sibling. Protection. You love this small, weak, crying, milk-stained grub, and it needs to be protected. Your parents are obviously the protectors, but they need you not to see the new arrival as a threat to the family ecosystem, so they teach you that you have to look after this new addition. That becomes your mission.

Which is weird, considering as an older sibling you'll spend most of your time beating the ever-loving shit out of your parents' other children. At this point I should point out, although I shouldn't actually have to, I never beat up

Josie. It wasn't that I couldn't take her. It wasn't even that I knew it was wrong. I just wouldn't. She never stepped out of line. She was just this immaculate being that you wanted to see smile, because that smile would change your entire day.

Then one day it didn't.

People have a tendency to get weird when you talk about death. Especially when dealing with family members. Even more so when you make fun of it. Which doesn't make much sense, seeing as death is the only thing we all have in common as human beings. And not just human beings. Dogs, too. And cats. Spoiler alert.

Sure, you'll meet some positive-thinking losers, those morons that have "Love, Laugh, Live" painted on their sexless bedroom wall, who will tell you that we all have "LOVE" or "HOPE" in common. They're wrong. Sociopaths can't feel love and Scottish football fans can't feel hope (much like Knicks fans, he says, pretending to understand the American sports reference his editor made him put in). The only thing we truly have in common is that we're all going to die one day. Race ya. Last one there is the loneliest.

Not only are you going to die, every person you've ever loved is going to die if they haven't already. Sound sad? It is. Not only is it sad, some of these deaths will fuck you up big time. I'm terrified of the day that one of my parents dies. I've already romanticized the alcohol-and-drug-fueled breakdown that I'll inevitably have. How I'll spend years failing to recover from it, hiding it from loved ones who

I slowly push away before I finally find the inner strength from a DMT-induced vision of my mother telling me to "Stop being such a baby," which is unlike her, but poignant nonetheless. Then I'll write a stand-up show about it. A stand-up show that wins me all the awards. But none of the plaudits will ever fill the void that Mummy hasn't prepared me for. The only death that isn't going to suck is our own, because we won't realize we're dead.

Want some good news, though? Everyone who is shit is also going to die. How brilliant is that? Every scientologist is going to die. Wonderful. Racists are going to die! And they're going to die miserable. Double whammy. Fuck, yes! Piers Morgan is going to die. Which will absolutely suck for his wife, kids, and the people that knew him. But what a day on Twitter we'll all have.

Death doesn't discriminate. Hitler died. Nelson Mandela died. Putin is going to die. Babies die. That's awful. Every single member of Hanson is going to die. Your high school bully is going to die. Sure, he's grown, matured, and doesn't remember the time he slapped the can of Coke out of your hands on the playground, let alone isn't aware of how you harbored this resentment for years and years and let it fuel you. He has kids now. Ugly kids. Kids who he loves and teaches to not bully other people, because he knows it's wrong. All that growth, yet still going to die. Justice is served, Jeff.

I'm actually quite excited for the Queen dying. Not in your typical Scottish "I didn't fucking vote for her, hashtag not my bloody Queen" way. I hate the monarchy, but even I can admit that Big Liz is a bit of a legend and a literal KWEEN. I'm just excited about the prospect because I'll get to be alive when they change the money and stamps. That'll be interesting. Whose head is it next? Will the heads face the same way? If the heads face opposite ways, does making them kiss count as treason? England will have to change its national anthem. Can't sing "God Save the Queen" after she dies. Bit rude. I just reckon it's going to be an interesting few months. That's all.

Death is the most common thing in the world, yet people still get uncomfortable around it. People don't know how to talk about it. What to say or how to say it. I don't mind talking about death or being blasé about it, because nothing I could ever say can be as painful as losing someone you love. I'm not more powerful than death. Not yet, anyway. Soon.

When people get upset about my casualness and dismissiveness of death, they're upset because they think I don't give a shit about the person in their life that died. They're right. I don't. Spot-on assessment, bee-tee-dubs.* They're dead and I didn't know them. Why would I give a shit? I'm sad that you're sad. I'm not a sociopath. I've got empathy coming out the wazoo. But their lack of breathing doesn't directly affect me, so why would I give an actual, real-life fuck?

---

* This is hip youth slang for BTW = by the way, old man.

I don't expect you to care about my sister, either. You didn't know her. You didn't hug her. You didn't make her laugh. She was my sister. Not yours. My grief. Back the fuck off. You can be empathetic. We all can. But don't turn empathy into a competition. I'll cry you under the table, bitch. That's what it can feel like when you lose someone close to you. Everyone suddenly races to tell you that they feel the most sorry, that they miss them, too, or that they know what you're going through. No, you fucking don't.

There are an infinite number of things that I hate about my sister's death. Near the top of the list has to be "mentioning it." Watching people not knowing what to say or do. Worried how to react. Whether to laugh at my jokes about it. It's so uncomfortable, and not because of me. The person who is grieving is never the one to make shit awkward. It's the emotionally stunted grief vultures that surround the grieving party saying shit like, "Let's watch TV but don't put on *Sister, Sister*. That might set him off." (An actual thing said in earshot of me after my sister died.)

Would you like to know what grieving people want you to say to them? Nothing. Because there is nothing that you can say to make things better. Nobody knows what the perfect thing to say after a death is. I do know the second-best thing to say, though. I know the only truly helpful thing you can say to someone when they're grieving. You ready?

Ahem.

"That's shit, mate."

It's the only honest thing you can say. It's shit. When

people die—it is shit. Doesn't sound like much, but I'd bet my house that it'll have a more positive effect than "I know what you're going through."

Feel free to improv with that, too, mix it up. Add some pizzazz. "Holy shit, that sucks a giant scrot!" or "Fucking hell, that's fucking shit and awful" or "What a shitter of a day."

Then sit down with them and talk about how fucking shit it is. Because it is. Death sucks.

Grieving people don't want to feel better. We want to grieve. To sit down and shout and cry. Throw a tantrum and complain about how unfair it is. I don't want to be told I'll feel better. I don't want to be told "It's all right." I especially don't want to be told that she's looking down on me. She isn't. She's dead, and thanks to my parents not being gullible, weak-willed, or unable to deal with complex emotions, I was not raised to think that death is a big fun prank that God plays before we all get to turn around in the giant ballpark in the sky, but not with the Muslims, Jews, or gays.

If you want to pray for me, do it out of my earshot. I'd rather hang out with the people who are actually trying to help, rather than people who are trying to make themselves feel better because they belong to a religion that is designed to stunt or prevent grief by promising you a future reunion that isn't ever going to happen. Your dead family members are dead and they don't miss you. Why? Because they're dead. Sorry, babe.

Sometimes the way to make someone feel better is by not trying to make them feel better. Let people be sad. It's not your job to fix them.

That's enough about death for now. I just had to bring it up because this chapter is about siblings. It would be a bit rude for me to not mention Jocelyn Christine Farty-pants Sloss.

If you don't have siblings, you're fucked. Statistically. Only children are the worst, man. Genuine pricks. You don't grow up with fear. Not true fear. Have you ever had the shit beaten out of you at one in the morning because you didn't put your older brother's Xbox controller back on to charge? Me neither. But my younger brothers have, and it looks rough.

I think siblings are incredibly important. They teach you a valuable lesson—sometimes you have to love people that you don't want to. Tough shit. They came out of the same pussy as you did, so get used to their faces because family is for life, not just for Christmas. I spent years of my life not wanting to love my brothers. Why would I? They were probably just going to die like my sister did. No point getting attached.

Sound harsh? It is. That's genuinely what went through my head as a kid. I was eight when my six-year-old sister died. An older brother has one job—to protect his younger siblings (while also regularly prescribing cans of whoop ass, to be taken orally every other day). Josie died. I failed to protect her. Bad big brother.

No one told me this, by the way. This isn't a rule I read somewhere. My parents certainly didn't say it to me. It manifested itself in my head. Whether that was through TV shows or books I have no idea. I just remember that my job was to protect her and thinking that I had failed. Josie died of natural causes, and there's nothing I could have done to prevent her death. I know that now. That's one of the advantages to being older, being able to look back at your childhood objectively and realizing, "Oh, holy shit. That fucked me up."

I have an older-brother complex now. After Josie went to that farm where all the other siblings go to that we're not allowed to visit because it's very far away, my aunt popped out her first kid. A daughter. And then another. I grew very close to my cousins, Eilidh* and Sara. I love them dearly. I was subconsciously replacing Josie. This also led me to not wanting to get too close to my brothers. Out of fear of getting attached and then losing them. Much easier to just never love them than run the risk of being sad about death again.

I was a bad big brother for years. The age gap between me and Matthew is ten years, and twelve for Jack. When I was thirteen, they were three and one, and they were proper little shits. I can't stress to you how much I thought I hated these little rats. I was filled with testosterone and rage and I hadn't really worked out what wanking was for yet. I was a hormone-ridden ball of anger.

* What I wouldn't give to watch you Americans try to pronounce this name.

But boy, did my brothers love me. I couldn't do anything to stop them from loving me. Believe me, I tried. They loved me with that unconditional love that children have.* I couldn't handle their love, so I just kept being horrible to them, in the hopes that they'd stop. They didn't.

I've been told by my family that I vilified Matthew far too much when we were younger, and I probably did. But I wasn't all bad.

Here is a true story. You be the judge. When Matthew was two, he had a lot of dummies. Or pacifiers, for you Yanks. *Pacifier,* as a word, really makes me laugh. They're called dummies in the UK because they're essentially dummy nipples. "Mummy's nipple is too sore, suck on this dummy one." Boom. Named dummies. Americans, you call them pacifiers like you're RoboCop. "I shall pacify the child. The baby has been pacified. No casualties. Beep boop beep."

Matthew kept fifty of these things in a bucket that he carried around everywhere. Unfortunately, he had the lexicon of a two-year-old. For some reason he couldn't say "dummies." He could only call them "me's." Whether this was learned narcissism from me or his baby diary was so full that he simply didn't have the time to say the first half of words, we'll never know. The point is he carried his "me's" around in this little bucket, swapping them out and mixing them up. Taking out one, inspecting it, and then

* Which we think is cute, but it isn't. They'd literally die without us. Sometimes even with. Exhibit A: Author gestures to this chapter.

comparing it to the one already in his thick little mouth. If it was deemed better, into his gob it went.

One day I'm on the couch watching *Sister, Sister* (and not being triggered, thank you very much). Matthew waddles in with his fat toddler arse and his "me bucket" and looks at me. I flip him off. Because he's two, he doesn't know what that means. Maybe he'll learn it from me and do it to Gran at some point. That'd be funny.

He didn't react. His beady little eyes just sized me up. He took his dummy out of his mouth and passed it to me. Like an olive branch. I wasn't completely deaf to my parents' requests to be nicer to Matthew, to try and be a positive role model in his life. Here was the actual son of Satan himself, offering me something that he loved and valued. If I positively reinforced this behavior, who knows what could happen. Maybe he'd become nicer. Maybe I could train him to give me everything he got for his birthday and then train him to ask for cool shit. The possibilities were endless.

I graciously accepted his gift of a saliva-coated Thomas the Tank Engine gob socket, patted him on the head, and said, "Thank you, Matthew. That was very nice of you." *You Pavlov's dog piece of shit.* I saw an instant reaction. He smiled, stared, and then—I cannot fucking stress to you how true this is—this little bitch calculated. As a two-year-old. I saw numbers and symbols behind his eyes as he did some very quick maths. He then handed me the entire bucket of dummies. Every last one. My younger brother, who was so horrible and evil, was doing something kind because he loved me. He was not only willing to share, but to give up his treasure trove of bacteria. All because his calculation added up to the fact that it made me happy. My heart warmed. I accepted the bucket and said again, "Thank you, Matthew."

Then this asshole looked at me. No dummy in his mouth. Shit-eating grin in full sight, only to me. He looked at the bucket of dummies. He looked at me. He looked at his dummy-less hands. I realized his plan one second too late. He screamed the bloody house down. Oh, my word. That first inhale of breath was so big my ears popped. My mum comes running into the room, sees a crying two-year-old with no dummies and a twelve-year-old older brother holding all of the dummies and she puts two and two together to make twelve. To this day she doesn't believe my version of events. Which is why it's now in this book that will be stored in the nonfiction section of a bookshop.

After Matthew came Jack. He seemed nice as a baby. We bonded a bit. Didn't have much in common. I'd still not fully hit puberty, I was struggling with my confidence (especially since everyone else was having their growth spurts while I was still five foot), girls didn't know I existed, and I liked computer games. Whereas Jack couldn't hold his head up and liked having my mother's tit in his mouth. Maybe that explains why my dad got on with him better.

In my head they had formed a team against me. Two little shits hell-bent on making my life miserable. In actual fact they just wanted my attention, and if they couldn't get it through love, they sure as hell could get it by being annoying. We had some good times and we had plenty of bad ones. I was too young and stupid to see the truth.

The way I treated my brothers when I was young fills me with guilt every single day. Well, not every single day. That would be exhausting. Once a month, maybe. It's nice to be dramatic. All they wanted to do was to love me and for me to love them, and I didn't, because I was scared. I robbed them of one of the most important characters in their lives, their older brother. I felt so bad about it for so long. It ate at me.

Then, two years ago, I got shitfaced with my brothers. (Yes, underage. This is Scotland. Grow up.) I poured my heart and soul out to them. Apologizing for the way I had treated them, the regret I felt, the guilt that consumed me.

Turns out the little shits don't remember any of it. Not a single fucking incident. They think I was, and still am, an excellent older brother. I literally cried about how awful it must have been for them and they both looked at me, blank-faced, and said, "What are you talking about? You were a great older brother!" Fucking idiots. Honestly. You try to emotionally scar people for life and this is how they repay you?

I don't know what my point is with that story. Maybe

it's that things aren't as bad as they seem. Or that we all perceive things differently. Or maybe it's if you hit your siblings hard enough, they'll forget the fact that you hit them. I genuinely don't know and I don't know if books are allowed to not have answers by the final edit.

I think we try to teach everyone this lie—that you have to love your family. I took that lesson and it worked for me. I've now got my two younger brothers, who I genuinely love and no longer beat the shit out of. Not because I don't want to, but because both of them got my dad's height and I got my mum's nose. That's fair. They could both beat my ass now.

Your family could suck. I've got mates with shit family members. Looks rough. Some family members can be toxic, parasitical, vindictive, or spiteful, and we teach ourselves that we have to forgive these personality traits because "that's your family." I respectfully disagree. I love my father with every fiber of my being, but if he was a big, vindictive bully who made my mother sad, I'd get my two bigger younger brothers to help me kick his fucking head in. If my mother was cruel and tried to upset me and my brothers so that she could feel better about herself, I wouldn't turn up for Christmas.

"Blood is thicker than water" is not only wrong as a sentiment, it's also wrongly quoted. The full proverb is "The blood of the covenant is thicker than the water of the womb." Which means the bonds you make through choice are infinitely more important and powerful than the ones you share by blood. Just because yer maw* shagged the same bloke twice and popped out another prick who has your eyes doesn't mean he should matter more to you than the lifelong friend you have.

I don't have an older brother, by blood. I do have a best friend, Kai, who is like an older brother to me in that he buys me drugs. Kidding. Well, not really, he does buy me drugs. I just mean that there is more to it than that. My other best friend, Jean, is like a sister to me. Except alive.

I don't think it's the people that matter. I think it's the role they play. Being an older brother taught me to protect people, to look out for people that I loved even when I didn't feel like loving them at that point in time. I was never a younger brother, so I didn't learn the lessons that they learn, such as "Plug my controller back in after you use it or I'll go Full Metal Jacket on your bitch ass."

Just because I wasn't born with an older sibling didn't mean I didn't yearn for it. Most of the friends that I have in my life are older than I am. I look up to them and I ignore every single bit of advice they give me, but I pretend to listen because I know what it's like to be a role model without actually being one.

Because I lost my sister at a young age, I spent most of the rest of my life trying to fill that role with multiple people, trying to become an "older brother" to women. Which is awful. Don't do that. That's a creepy thing that

---

* Some of this book will remain in Scottish and I'll translate as I go. "Yer maw" = your mother.

creeps do and it usually doesn't make women feel any safer. You don't get to nominate yourself to be someone's relative, you psycho.

I dunno what I'm getting at here. This feels like more of a cathartic chapter than anything else. I tried to write a chapter on my relationship with my siblings, but I actually think it's been a chapter about my relationship with death. In the Venn diagram of my life, those things overlap more than I'd like. I guess the point I'm trying to make is, if I could give any advice to my younger self, it would be to be a better sibling. Which doesn't even make sense, because apparently I was a good one.

Death robs you of answers. Sometimes it doesn't let you finish the question. It's so fucking common and it is as old as time itself, yet we still don't know how to deal with it. I think that's why I hate religion so much. Jealousy. It must be so great to believe in an afterlife. To think that your grandparents are playing cribbage on a porch on the clouds while Jesus pops over asking to borrow a cup of sugar and to say they're just waiting for you to turn up. That somewhere up there, my sister is waiting. She can walk and talk and she is just biding her time until I show up so she can reassure me that I was a good big brother. That I did do everything I could. That she loved me and she watched my show *Dark* and loved the way I spoke about her. She'd make jokes about how her dying made me a better person. Brought me closer to my parents. Made me a better comedian. Made me who I am today. That she doesn't resent any of that.

That she's happy and I made her happy. It would be nice to believe that.

But I don't.

I believe that she's gone in every single way apart from memory. Psychologists among you might point out that she left scars, too. I have no idea. I believe that when we die, nothing happens. I don't even believe it. I am certain of it. There is no God. There is no heaven. There is no afterlife. There is no higher consciousness. Souls are utter bollocks and don't even get me started on karma.

It doesn't upset me, though. It makes me appreciate life way more. The chances of you existing are statistically impossible. Billions upon trillions to one. Your parents had to fuck at the exact right moment for you to exist, otherwise you'd be a different egg, a different sperm, a different person. For your parents to exist, your grandparents had to rail each other at the exact moment they did. If your granddad had faked an orgasm or your gran decided to take a load to the tits, then your dad wouldn't be your dad and you wouldn't be you.

That goes on and on and on and on for generations. We are a statistical anomaly floating on a rock through an infinite space. A space so infinite that even our infinite minds are incapable of processing the very idea of the infinity we inhabit. We're so terrified of how small and unimportant we are that we create gods and heavens and hells and stories of fantasy to make us feel like we matter when none of us do. We don't matter to the universe. We don't matter to Earth. I find comfort in that. Nothing in the universe matters, yet I matter to someone. People matter to me. We matter to one another. Sometimes more than we realize.

I really don't know if this chapter will make it to the book, boys and girls. I'm not even sure if I want it in here. It started dark and then ended waaaaay darker. It's definitely going to make my mum cry, and that's never fun.

When I toured my show *Dark,* which was about Josie's death (streaming on Netflix worldwide. The show. Not her death.) I really learned how good it was to talk about deaths that had affected you. I also learned that a lot of people like to listen to people talk about death, because we don't do it enough. We hide it. We ignore it. We make it taboo, and I think that gives it too much power. So if you're like me and you think this chapter was a bit too dark and personal, I get it. Let's move on to the next chapter together. But I hope that for some of you, this made sense. That the uncertainty I felt while typing it perhaps clicked something into place for you. In a world where we strive to be different, to stand out, to be unique and not be like anyone else, sometimes it's nice to know that we aren't different. We are the same. We're all scared little apes burdened with thoughts, worries, and uncertainty. Even our fight to be different proves how we're the same. Christ, I sound like a fucking hippie.

I loved being a brother to Josie and I love being a brother to whatever the other two are called. Being a sibling is forced love, and even though that sounds awful, I don't think it is. If you are a sibling, relish that. I truly believe it's a close bond (although that doesn't mean you shouldn't cut the cunts out of your life if they're toxic as shit. More on toxic relationships later).

If you're an only child, just resign yourself to the fact that you're broken on the inside. You are categorically not capable of the same love as the rest of us. I became a pseudo-parent at the age of two. You were a child until your parents decided you weren't. You are less tolerant. You are less understanding. You are less lovable.

And if that upsets you, what the actual fuck are you going to do about it? Get your older sibling on me?

I don't know if "My older brother will batter you" exists in countries outside of Scotland, but I hope it does. I had never been able to threaten enemies with a larger version of myself until I met Kai. But I was used as that threat many times. And being ten years older than Matthew and twelve years older than Jack made confrontations interesting.

I was sixteen years old, playing World of Warcraft in my bedroom. Suddenly, Jack bursts into my room shouting and screaming. Normally this would warrant me yelling at him because one day this might not be World of Warcraft I'm watching, but porn downloaded from LimeWire (big shout-out to you '90s kids who killed your computers in the search for porn).

Jack starts telling me about how Matthew has gotten into some argument with some kid across the road, and the kid is threatening to beat Matthew up. I'm currently trying to do an Onyxia speed run without a Paladin (I know), so

I'm not interested. This doesn't deter Jack; he keeps explaining the predicament. In order to shut him up I casually say, "Tell any kid threatening Matthew that I'll kick his fucking head in" (to anyone outside Scotland this might sound unusual, but trust me: standard).

Upon hearing this, Jack is filled with joy. His hero big brother has saved the day. He runs out the front door like a town crier, "Hear ye, hear ye! He who layeth a hand upon mine older brother shall feel the wrath of my eldest brother." The eight-year-olds who are threatening Matthew flee in fear at the thought of my rage. They go to get their big brother for the famed "brother fight."

Naturally, with Matthew's tormentor being eight years old, the older brother was only eleven. He confidently turned up at my front door to beat me up. He'd done the maths— his brother was eight, my brother was six. He must be at least two years older than me. Easy fight.

WRONG, SHITEBAG.

The fear on this kid's face was almost not visible as I beat him to within an inch of his life for daring to touch my brother. I don't know if you've ever unleashed the fury of all your pent-up, teenage, virgin hormones onto the hairless face of a baby ned (Scottish scum), but it's quite fulfilling.

I'm kidding! I've never been in a fight in my life.

The big brother turned up at the front door, asked for me, met me, reassessed the situation, and then fucked off promptly. Not because I was stronger than he was. But because I was six years older with two mates as well. Alone, he probably could've taken me. He doesn't know that, though.

That being said, I did wallop Matthew around the ear for nearly getting me into danger. That'll teach him.

Chapter 3

Genitalia: Our Best Friends and Our Worst Enemies

I'm not really sure when I lost my virginity. I tried to with a young lady when I was seventeen, but I don't think stubbing your toe on someone's front steps counts as breaking and entering. It's barely even property damage.

I remember counting it as sex at the time. Despite the fact that zero penetration happened, I concluded that because a girl had consented to having sex and we'd done our best, that absolutely counted as *having* sex. Everything else was just semantics. Look, if you go to Disneyland and are too short to get on the rides, you can still tell people that you went to Disneyland. Would you tell a dying nine-year-old that she hadn't been to the fabled theme park because they wouldn't let her on Splash Mountain? No. I thought not.

I think there are two types of teenagers. Those that see their virginity as something special and those that see it as a disease. One half sees having sex as losing something special they'll have only once, while to the rest of us it is more like having baby teeth. Sure, it made sense to have them when you were young, but at twenty-three you'd just look weird.

I fell into the second category. Sex was something cool people did. I wanted to be cool, ergo, having sex would make me cool. I really do wish life was as simple as I used to think it was. I don't know how I thought that worked. The only way people would know you'd had sex was if you told them, and the one thing we all know from high school is that the kid who says he's getting laid is very much the kid who is not even close to getting laid.

Eventually I had real sex. I think it was a few months after take one, the drunken crotch jousting of two awkward teens. I was stone-cold sober the second time, so everything went where it was meant to end up. This time it was less like trying to get a sleeping bag back into its case.

I don't think your first time matters too much. But at the time, it's one of the most important things in the world. Then you get out of high school and realize that the rest of the world doesn't give a fuck about your life or your genitals, unless you're a woman in Georgia. In which case your body is obviously property of the United States government. Just as God intended.

I'm not a big believer in this "your first time should be special" bollocks. My first time wasn't that special and I've turned out to be a perfectly functioning alcoholic whore with a God complex. The first time I have ever done anything has always ended up being an absolute disaster.

That's how all first attempts should go. You should never be instantly good at something. Especially sex.

I think it's good if your first time is with someone you know well and trust, but let's not build sex up to be this life-changing, groundbreaking, love-making, sacred act of two bodies joining together in naked unity, allowing their souls to intertwine, blah blah blah. Too much buildup completely ruins everything. Nobody wants to be the sexual equivalent of season eight of *Game of Thrones*.

It's the difference between doing stand-up in America and in the UK. In America the host introduces acts like this: "You have seen this guy on YouTube, he's a regular host at the Chunk Monkey Barrel of Laughs, and you may have seen him as background nerd number four, it's . . ." and then they bring on some guy who is hugely underwhelming despite his fake impressive CV. The bar is set too high. It's the opposite in the UK. We're of the "Don't even tell them he's a comedian, let them work it out; if they don't, he's not" school.

Sex can be the greatest thing in the world. It can feel like time has stopped and nothing else in the world matters apart from your depraved antics. It can also last five minutes and be done mostly as a favor. Neither is wrong in my book. Potato tomato.

Don't make teenagers think sex is going to change their lives. It's already terrifying for them. That's where the fear of "Oh, God, I have to lose it, otherwise I'm a freak" comes from. Teenagers are already going through enough. Your body starts going through these changes. Things you've never felt before start taking over every waking thought you have. You notice different things about yourself. About your classmates. About your teachers.

You're suddenly horny, but you don't know what horny is. That's confusing, to say the least. Imagine having never needed to eat in your life. You absorb shit from the sun or whatever, I dunno, you work out the science. Then at the age of thirteen you suddenly start growing a stomach. Small at first, but over time it grows. You have no idea what's happening. There's just suddenly this empty, gnawing feeling in your gut. It's hunger. But you've never been hungry before. You've not even eaten. You've heard of food, obviously. You've seen people with food in movies and you've heard stories about Stephen's big brother, who apparently has bagels all the time, but he got them from a different school. Now it's happening to you and you don't really know how to remedy it.

At this point the school starts to realize the fact that most of you are drawing avocado on toast in the back of your schoolbooks and there are rumors going around that a couple of kids ate finger foods over the weekend. The principal decides it's best to start teaching you about cooking and food safety. There's a class on the dangers of food poisoning, but there's never a class on how to cook an egg. They'll teach you most things *about* food, but they won't teach you how to actually *cook*. They teach you the science of cooking, how it works, and how your body turns it into shit. And your teacher says that if she catches you watching Gordon Ramsay videos in class again you'll be sent to detention.

Then the Church turns up and starts telling you that most food is a sin. Not only that. Cooking only for yourself is one of the worst things you can do (outside of shoving a panini straight up your shitter). And, of course, we're all constantly cooking for ourselves. It's the only way to stop being so hungry. You eat all the time when you're alone. You're upstairs in your room, door locked, hunched over the table, ramming dry cereal down your throat because you haven't discovered the joys of milk yet. Suddenly your mum shouts and tells you that it's time for you to come down and have sex with your family. I've lost the analogy, but we can all agree that it was good up until then.

When we're in our teens we're already the most awkward, unsure versions of ourselves that we're going to be, walking around trying to desperately fit into this small subsection of society instead of making sure that we're emotionally prepared for the real version. After high school we have to work out what we want to do, where we want to do it, how we're going to afford it, who our friends are going to be, how the fuck we work out what to tip in restaurants. Stop ruining sex for teenagers! It's all they have.

Have as much sex as you can when you're young, because it's the only time you're allowed to suck at it. It doesn't even have to be with multiple people. If that's not your flavor of ice cream, then so be it, but you can still have a lot of sex with one individual. It's why I think fuck buddies are an incredibly important part of growing up and becoming an adult. While you focus on your job, your social life, your university work, and all the other stresses of life, sometimes you don't need the complexities of a relationship coming into the mix. But we all need sex. Find a like-minded individual who will let you bleed the radiator together. Practice on each other. Try things out on each other that you normally wouldn't try out. You'll learn things about yourself. Sometimes things you wish you never knew. There are few things worse than discovering you're a pervert. That drunken moment at four a.m. when your inebriated brain "accidentally" clicks on *that* porn tab and you suddenly realize, "Fuck, I'm into that."

It's possible to have sex with people and not marry them. It's also important to note that just because someone fucks you doesn't mean they think that you are husband or wife material. Sometimes sex is just fun. Stop trying to ram emotions into everything. There's making love and then there is fucking. Two entirely different forms of sex.

Making love is nice and beautiful, the birds sing, deer clap their hooves as they watch from the shrubbery, and a rainbow fires out of your arsehole and projects the images of your future children onto the ceiling with potential baby names and a list of the best local schools.

Fucking is more carnal. It's instinctive. It occasionally leaves bruises, scratches, and other marks. It's proper cardio.

In fact, it's the only cardio most of us enjoy and can stick to. I'd be much better on a treadmill if it meant that if I stopped running, even for a second, the treadmill would stop entirely, then go around and tell all the other treadmills that I need better running shoes.

Making love is what you do with people with whom you have a deep, emotional bond. Someone you can talk to for hours on end and to whom you bare your soul. Fucking is for people who you just have to fuck. People who you have nothing in common with other than the fact that you both want to fuck each other within eight and a half inches of your lives.

You need both. Without fucking, lovemaking wouldn't be special. If everything is making love, then nothing is making love. You can't make love doggy-style. Lovemaking requires eye contact. Having your partner hold on to a wing mirror while you plow into the back of her doesn't suddenly mean you can put Barry White on and call it Valentine's Day. This theory applies strictly to heterosexual sex. If you're having gay sex, in this particular instance you're on your own.

Sex can still be special if you sleep around, too. Some people live under the impression that if you spend most of your life fucking, you get bored with it or you ruin it for yourself. Not true. You've always got lovemaking. Nobody makes love the first time. Not since World War Two and the whole "I ship out in the morning" shtick still existed has anyone ever made love on the first go. Too big a gamble.

Understand, I don't think waiting for the right person and having sex with only her or him is a bad thing. I think it's great. If that's what you're about. I also don't believe having lots of sex with a bunch of people makes you any less of a person than the other ones. Each to his or her own.

You'll meet people who will proudly boast that they've only ever had sex with one person. Good for them. It must be bliss having a partner who has nothing to compare it to. Someone who doesn't have a large palate. Porridge must be the greatest thing in the world when you've never heard of chocolate. People who say "My body is a temple" seriously underestimate how many people visit temples.

"My partner has only ever had sex with me." Cool. Enjoy mediocrity together. I'm sure your kids will be thrilled to hear the story of their conception: "Ah, yes, your mother had just finished her chardonnay and turned off *The Big Bang Theory.* She had that glint in her eye. That same one she gets when she sees me taking the garbage out when she hasn't even asked. She turned off the bedroom light and we had four minutes of missionary. At one point I touched her breast. We showered separately afterward and the next day I went to confession. Nine months later, you were born."

My future wife is out there right now, sucking as much dick as she wants. She's getting proper good at it, too. You go get it, future mother of my kids. Have the time of your life, sweetheart. I'll see you soon. Brush your teeth. Love you.

I don't know if you've ever had sex with a virgin, but they are awful at it. I know because I was awful long after I was a virgin. And I thank every woman who took time out of her very busy schedule to make me less of a physical embarrassment. Virgin sex is all very elbowy and grunty and involves more apologies than a British funeral. I don't want that to be my wife. We go out for years. Save our bodies because of God. Finally get married, head upstairs, take our clothes off, and just look at each other with the same amount of confusion as two stoners with an IKEA flatbed and no instruction manual.

You'll find some people who get jealous of their partner's past sexual conquests. I imagine these people also get into rental cars, look at the mileage, and mutter, "You fucking slut, Cadillac," under their breath. These people can play only in the snow that's not been disturbed. They refuse to eat peanut butter unless they're the one who stuck the knife in first. They refuse to hold their firstborn because the doctor held it before they did.

I don't recommend being in a relationship with someone who gets jealous about that sort of shit. It's toxic and it puts you on the back foot for the entire relationship as you attempt to apologize for decisions you made well before you were aware the other person existed.

"I can't believe you've had sex with that many people." Dude, I only found out you were an option six months ago. Chill the fuck out. I flew EasyJet until I could afford British

Airways. I'm a big believer that anything you do before you meet your partner doesn't count (as long as it's legal, obviously) and they shouldn't hold it against you.

My ex-girlfriend used to use my past against me all the time. Whenever she saw or met someone that I'd had sex with she'd point out how disgusting it was, that I was still hanging around with them. As if that's all they were, "people Daniel has had sex with," as opposed to human beings and friends that I happened to have been intimate with years ago.

Jealous people make you feel like property. That's because that's what you are to them. You're not a person. You're a trophy. A medal. Something they can flaunt and boast about. They see your past as something dangerous, because it didn't involve them. They try to make you feel ashamed that you lived a life before they existed. They do it so much that you hate the idea of yourself not being with them because you'll be reduced back to the subhuman that you once were, at least in their eyes.

These jealous losers exist because for their entire life they were taught that sex was something special and unique. Something to participate in only during the right moonlight and while you're facing east. They think that the act is now diminished or lessened by experience. They put shagging on such a high pedestal you have to get on your tippy-toes to go down on it.

I don't want that in a partner. For the same reasons I don't want to get on an airplane and hear the pilot say, "I saved my first flight for you guys." Fuck that, take some lessons. Fly a few solo missions and I'll see you when you've got your wings.

I don't think you should have sex for the sake of it. Unless, of course, you want to. I just think having a healthy relationship with sex is crucial to your development as a human being. The way we're taught about sex is often damaging in the long term and can take years to unlearn. Traditionally, whether it's intentional or not, we're taught that men should be the ones trying to *get* sex. The chasers. The ones that enjoy sex and want to have it as much as possible, while women are the gatekeepers of sex. This perpetuates all those stereotypes that men have to earn sex and that a woman who gives it up easily is lesser than other women who have tighter thighs. I think we should teach kids that sex isn't an achievement or a goal. It's not something you have to coax someone out of. Or something that you should hold on to and hide.

It's a fun activity and it's good only when both of you want to play it. No one wants to play tennis with someone who doesn't want to play. That's just one of you pinging balls at someone trying to have a picnic. You wouldn't enjoy that game, because your partner's heart isn't in it. And you wouldn't plead, insist, or force them to play. It's supposed to be fun. Just because someone is dressed for tennis doesn't mean he or she wants to play tennis, and that person doesn't owe you a game of tennis just because you've played together before.

Maybe it's a generational thing. I don't know how it worked back when my grandparents were young. Wandering down to your local discotheque, hitting a wooden wheel with a stick, ration card hanging out of your top pocket, hoping to find a dame who wants to split half a bar of dark chocolate behind the local YMCA. Or the next generation that followed, being too young to contribute anything to the war but still wanting the same respect as those who actually fought the Nazis. You know, Boomer shit.

I don't care what any pensioner says, dating back then was just plain wrong. Every old person's story of how they met their wife goes, "Well, she didn't actually like me at first, but I wore her down." Ahh, yes, the romance of Stockholm syndrome. How easy it must have been to fall in love when there were only fifty options because travel hadn't been invented yet.

I feel my generation is mostly quite liberal when it comes to sex. That could be a somewhat skewed perspective, seeing as I don't hang out with many Americans. No offense, America, but you are, whether you like it or not, a Christian nation. We all know how well religious freedom and sexual freedom get on together.

If it appears that I'm shaming people who don't have a lot of sex, I am. These are the people that tend to slut-shame. They project their insecurities onto others. Anyone else who is having lots of sex must be doing it for attention. Because nothing draws as much attention as one-on-one activities.

The most important thing to remember about slut-shaming is that it requires two things: being a slut and being ashamed. I may be a slut, but I sure as hell am not ashamed. I'll fuck both your parents so good and proper that they'll leave each other. Drop the 'tude, Claire. I'm safe, I'm clean, I'm respectful, and I'm a lot more fun in a game of "Never have I ever."

There was a point in my life when my goal was to have sex with more than a hundred people. All my friends had had so much sex and I hadn't. They were all "centurions" and I sat there having had sex only with both of my previous girlfriends and the awkward crotch high-five I'd done in my eighteenth year. I think I thought that if I had sex with a hundred people it would erase the memory of all the rejection and awkwardness of my teenage years. That's the male ego for you.

My justification was this: I believe the number-one cause of breakups, divorces, and adultery (apart from myself) is curiosity. People who get into relationships too young, who have sex with only that one person, by the time they get to their mid-thirties or forties they think, *Oh, my God, I've not really experienced as much as I should. I'm missing out.* Now, whether they are missing out is neither here nor there, but it's how they feel, so they cheat or they break up.

I believe all that can be avoided by having a joyous, slutty time in your late teens and all through your twenties. Have as much consensual sex as you possibly can, get good at it, find out what you like, and have a bloody good exploration of yourself and your body. Then, when you meet the right person, you can both fuck each other to your heart's content, knowing that you've found the best. No niggling curiosity in the back of your mind saying, "What would it be like if I was single?" Because you already thoroughly know. It was great, but it's not this.

My way of making sure I will have no curiosity has been to stay single and have sex if and when it was available. It wasn't an obsession, per se. More a filthy hobby. I wasn't going out every single night trying to fuck anything that moved. I was just looking for like-minded individuals who had the same outlook toward casual sex as I did.

This was all made much easier by the invention of Tinder. If you've never experienced Tinder, do not worry, its golden years are well and truly gone. It used to be the most incredible thing in the entire world. For men.

The app that was literally just for hookups. Just like-minded people, in their twenties, who liked banter, sex, and fun, and didn't want a relationship. All you had to do was download this little app and swipe away. The first woman I ever met on it was from Adelaide, Australia. We went out, had drinks, laughed for a couple of hours, and she suddenly went, "Shall we go have sex now?"

This blew my fucking mind. I still had a lot of my younger attitudes toward sex. In that I thought women didn't enjoy it. At least not as much as blokes did. It was something men wanted and women gave. Nature or whatever the fuck David Attenborough harps on about.

The actual truth was that women *didn't* enjoy sex with *me* as much as I enjoyed having sex with them, because I was shit at it. Men who think women don't enjoy sex, in their experience, are technically right. Every woman they've ever fucked hated it.

We went back to my hotel and had a great couple hours. My mind was blown. Hers was kept firmly together. The next morning, we had breakfast, I asked for her number, and she just looked at me and said, "Why?" I had no answer. She laughed, then disappeared into the utter, utter, utter shithole that is Adelaide.*

This continued to happen on most Tinder dates. You'd meet up, have a few drinks, see if you get on, and if you both liked each other, you both started dropping unsubtle hints and then you went and had consensual, safe sex with someone you'd met that same day. Sometimes the flings went on for a few days. If you had a connection, you'd meet up another night and do the same again. Proper, perfect little romances. Enough time to get to know someone, bond with them, and have little jokes together. But not enough time for you to wind them up, or for either of you to see behind the mask.

Every single one of these was like the first two months of a relationship. Where you're so blinded by lust and hormones and desire that the other person's gaping flaws

---

* There is no worse place on this planet than Adelaide, Australia. If everyone in Adelaide were to suddenly disappear, it would take humanity ten years to find out, and even then no one would give a shit.

seem quirky and manageable. You haven't hung around long enough for them to realize that you have only about seven stories, and once they've heard them all you're pretty much fucked.

There are few relationships that you can look back on and not regret parts of them. Normally, you fall in love with the idea of someone, the idea they have pitched to you. Their best self meeting your best self. As time goes on, their performance drops. As does your own charade. You see behind the curtain and it isn't what you thought was there. Or wanted to be there. You cut your losses and make your way to the next lie, in the hope that soon you'll find the person you no longer have to pretend in front of. The person who doesn't want the puppet, but prefers the carpenter. That person who loves you for who you really are, and you adore her very soul even though you know souls don't exist. It's very confusing. Love turns you into a fucking hippie and it sucks. With Tinder you just got the fun stuff.

If you're a woman, I imagine those previous few paragraphs made absolutely no sense to you, seeing as that is almost definitely not the online dating experience you have had. I'm very aware of that. On Tinder, as a man, all you had to do was not be a fucking psychopath and you were already better than 99 percent of the men on there. If the first thing you sent a girl was anything other than a dick pic, you absolutely exceeded her expectations. Women react very well to being treated like human beings and I recommend doing so, even when not trying to get laid.

Being on Tinder as a woman is a nightmare. As a bloke, dating apps are kind of like house viewing. You look through a few pictures, find one you could comfortably see yourself inside of, and then try your hardest to be the best option for that person.

Tinder for women is like *Deal or No Deal.* But in four of the boxes are rapists, ten of them are dick pics, one of them is your ex, two of them can't spell, and they all think they're God's gift to the world. It's a minefield I have never had to experience. I've met some insane women in my time online dating, but none that I ever feared would literally murder me if I rejected their sexual advances.

Tinder has become a cesspool of bad options because fun people kept telling their shit mates about it and now it's all been overrun by plebs. If you go around saying, "I'm not on here for a one-night stand," then I suggest you get the fuck off the one-night-stand app. You don't walk into a butcher shop and say "I'm not here for meat" and then expect the gentleman behind the bar to whip up a salad. Go to a salad bar and stop ruining the meat shop. There are hundreds of dating websites. Stick to them. We were all having the time of our lives until you came over here.

I'd love to tell you that while on my quest to have sex with a hundred people, I realized that it was an egotistical endeavor fueled by my misconception that sex leads to happiness and that sleeping with as many people as possible did nothing but temporarily fill the emptiness inside of me and that the feelings of joy became more fleeting as time went on as I slowly numbed myself to the experience of making love because I put too much value on quantity over quality.

Sorry. That didn't happen. I had an excellent couple of years. Met some of the best people I've ever met in my life, tried new things, had a lot of fun, and ended up with only one STD. Not even one of the bad ones. Just chlamydia. And koalas get that, so, if anything, I'm adorable. Although I did come to realize that my quest to have sex with a hundred people was egotistical and ultimately a bit pathetic. I worked that out at around number 102. I find it difficult to reflect honestly on that time in my life. I know my younger self's intentions weren't inherently cruel. Just misguided and a bit vapid. They still probably hurt people. As much as I say it was all fun and flings, I definitely put my own feelings and goals far ahead of others. That isn't a crime. But that doesn't mean it's morally right.

Sex is different for all of us. I'm a heterosexual man, so sex to me doesn't require much trust. For a man, the only things that can really go wrong having sex are that you get a disease, which can be prevented by wearing condoms; you get a girl pregnant, which can be prevented by wearing condoms; or you get your dick bitten off, which can be prevented by having a decent taste in human beings.

For women, having sex involves another person physically inside of your body. It's got to be the most trusting thing in the entire world. You're at your most vulnerable. You're naked, you're as open as can be, and there is another human being literally inside of you. I think men need to try and empathize with that a bit more. Look at how most heterosexual men react when you try to shove something up their arse. They freak out. They do understand body autonomy, but most of the time it's buried so deep down it takes finding their G-spot for them to become aware of it.

Men won't take this stuff into consideration not because they're assholes, but just because we weren't taught that. I had sex education when I was in high school, but everything I learned about sex I learned from *having* sex. I think sex education needs to not only be made compulsory around the world, the countries that currently have it need to improve theirs. The reason we're all awkward about sex the first time we have it is because you're making schoolteachers teach kids about sex.

Nobody wants to learn about sex from their fucking teachers. Teachers should remain sexless beings. It's an awkward situation for everyone. The teacher is awkward. The class is awkward. The videos are awkward. Is it any surprise that the first time we have sex also turns out to be awkward?

Without good sex education the only other place to really learn about sex is from porn, and that's not necessarily ideal. Now, I don't buy into this "Porn is harmful" black-and-white, no-room-for-debate narrative. I think, like most things, it can be dangerous in excess. That's what *excess* means. Even though some absolute cretins on the planet are unable to tell the difference between fantasy and reality, that doesn't mean the rest of us are going to watch porn and automatically think, *Women love fists up their arses with no warning.*

I think porn has made a positive contribution to the world as well. My generation was the first generation to have it available at the tip of our fingers whenever we want. We watched it from a younger age than our predecessors did, and so weren't as terrified of it. We were introduced to fetishes from a dropdown list as opposed to finding someone who was just into weird shit.

Back when I was young we used to get porn from Kazaa or LimeWire. If you don't know what these are, they were essentially the first-ever torrenting programs on computers in the 2000s. You'd download LimeWire and you just typed in what music, movie, TV show, or game you wanted on your computer, pressed enter, and it would give you a list of possible downloads. Ninety-five percent of these were either viruses that would absolutely destroy your computer or, occasionally, bestiality porn falsely named "I believe I can fly MPEG." Sound disgusting? It was. And it's incredible to think that now, thanks to what R. Kelly has done, bestiality is no longer the worst thing I associate with his name. The Internet was a lawless place before it turned into shit. Proper fun.

Sex is part of human life. It's something most of us experience. Your mum and dad fucked. Your grandparents fucked. They probably still do. There are [fill in your country's legal age] years of life where you shouldn't be having sex and then the rest of it is probably fair game as long as you aren't being a dick. I understand the theory that young minds need to be protected and that they're too young for some things. I also think that a lot of people are far too fucking old for the awkwardness they experience when it comes to sex.

The only reason taboo subjects exist is because people are too afraid to talk about them. The more, as a society, we talk about sex, the less awkward it will become. I'm not suggesting you phone up your parents and start comparing notes on sixty-nineing. Just accept the awkwardness, talk about it despite the fact that it's awkward, and watch everything get easier from there on in.

Chapter 4

Friends with the Opposite Bits

If you've ever seen my stand-up (or actually read all the pages up to this point), you'll have no doubt heard me talking about one of my best friends, Jean. You'll notice in this book I have a lot of best friends. I'm incredibly lucky in that sense, and I genuinely couldn't pick—among Ally, Jean, or Kai—who is my bestest friend. As it changes daily. Not in a nice way. Some days one of them will super piss me off, and silently in my head, every time they say something, I think, *Shut up, number three.* Always keep people on their toes.

Best friends are like children: Having more than one doesn't diminish your love for the others, but you'd be an outright liar if you said that you occasionally didn't have a favorite.

If you haven't seen my stand-up, I can't fathom why you would have this book on you right now. If I had to guess, I'd assume I was a Christmas stocking filler. Or a recommendation from someone you now fucking hate. I get it. I once had a friend recommend *The Great Gatsby.* We don't talk anymore. If Jean had recommended *The Great Gatsby*, I wouldn't be writing this chapter right now. I wouldn't even blink if I was told she had died.

God, I sincerely hope my publishers aren't big F. Scott Fitzgerald fans because this is a stance I will not be moved on.* Unlikely, though. The Venn diagram of people who read my book and people who like *The Great Gatsby* is just a pair of far apart, oddly sized breasts.

How you meet your friends often defines the rest of your friendship with them. If the first time you met your buddy was getting absolutely rat-arsed in a nightclub, chances are that most of the time you'll spend with him will be partying and trying to recapture those perfect first few months of friendship before his shitty personality bobs its way to the surface.

That's why we outgrow friends. As we get older, we change. Sometimes that causes us to see certain friends less, or we see them in entirely different scenarios and you realize you really liked only one aspect of them—they knew a reliable dealer in Edinburgh.

Sometimes you'll make a new friend and you'll think they're the best. They're funny, they're smart, they're adventu-

---

* I just think it's an awful book. Fawned over because it was considered in the top ten books when there were only thirteen books in existence. Older generations demanding it still be given the same respect as all the new books that involve things happening and interesting dialogue. "Oh, the sad millionaire doesn't know if people like him for him or his money." Who gives an actual fuck? Maybe I'm too stupid for *The Great Gatsby.* If so, nothing has made intelligence seem less appealing. I'd rather shit in my hands and clap.

rous. You want to see them more and more. You prioritize them. Include them in all of your plans. Then there's that horrible moment when you play with a toy too much and it breaks. You see them too drunk, or they open up a side of themselves that you hadn't seen before and ask you if you wouldn't mind reading their poetry (which is the lowest form of art after mime. And this is coming from a comedian). You suddenly think, *Oh, shit, this one is fucking mental. ABORT. ABORT!*

I think that's why we desperately hold on to some friends. They remind us of a different, younger, funner version of ourselves and we think, *If I keep reliving my youth, maybe it won't slip desperately away.*

The real secret is to simply be the same piece of shit you always were, just in classier situations. If I drink twenty pints and ten Jäger bombs in a nightclub, a lot of people are going to ask me if everything is all right at home. If I drink three bottles of wine and pick off a cheeseboard with four friends, I'm a connoisseur. You stick a candle in a Chianti bottle and you're a classy, trendy, recycling young gentleman. You stick a candle in a vodka bottle and you're a Ukrainian separatist desperately fighting off the Russians. And good on you.

That's why people that you've been friends with for a long time are that extra bit special. They survived all of your changes. You, in turn, survived theirs, you tenacious fuck. Look at you, not being expendable. Good job. Despite the differences and the distance between you both, you still have that one part of you that fully connects with each other and you know that it's too precious to lose.

It's an amazing thing to have a long-term friend. Someone who truly knows you. Someone who not only saw most of the incidents that made you the way you are, but who helped bring you back from the brink. Who led you in the right direction and who spoke the very uncomfortable truths that no one else had the balls to tell you.

I first met Jean when I was seventeen years old. I was at your typical underage drinking party in Scotland. Some teenager's parents had gone away for a weekend and trusted their child with an empty house. The naïveté of a lot of parents never fails to stun me. You know I'm not going to have a quiet weekend in an empty house for the same reason that I know you and Dad aren't going to a hotel in the Lake District because you like the scenery. It's because one of you found a new fetish and you don't want to Google "Can you tumble-dry latex?" on the family computer.

So we're at this party, destroying my friend's house and looking through his mum's drawers for her dildos. Teenage boys are bastards and there's not much you can do to change that. While I'm elbow deep in granny panties, I look up and see this gorgeous emo girl. She was confident. She was funny. She was smart. I found out all that later on in our relationship. The first thing I noticed was her tits. The first thing she noticed about me was that I cheered when I found a dildo. That must've been quite confusing for her, now that I think about it.

We attempted to flirt with each other in the way that teenagers awkwardly do. We drunkenly kissed around a fire in the garden while I pretended that I loved smoking while she pretended that she loved boys who smoke. Both of us emulating the sexy men and women we grew up watching on TV, hoping it was enough to convince the other to rub their genitals on ours. Ahhh, young love.

Anyway, eventually we shagged.* I liked that a lot. Big fan. Would recommend. This is why I don't respect nuns and neither should you. This girl and I started having sex more frequently. Typical of young lust: We ignored every gaping flaw in each other's personality for as long as possible so we could fuck forever.

One day she decided I should meet her best friend. Phase two. You always have to impress your partner's best friends. It's like being brought in front of a series of judges who decide the fate of your relationship. They bring you out and parade you in front of their closest friends. "Does this appease the coven?"

The coven looks down upon you, assessing your suitability. Are you nice enough? Are you attractive enough? Are you the right level of in love? Too little isn't good enough and too much is worrying. You really have to have the Goldilocks levels of lust for their "bestie." And you have to pretend that you don't want to fuck most of them.

It is crucial to impress these friends. They know your

---

* That's British for fucking. Seriously, do you have a passport? Have you gone anywhere but your local Denny's or IHOP?

partner way better than you do. Win them over and they'll be in your corner during the tough times. Piss them off and they are a cancerous mole on the balls of love life.*

She and I walked into the park, hand in hand, ready to meet the girl who was in charge of my sexual fate. On a roundabout in the middle of the park sat the gatekeeper. She had a mullet and was putting eyeliner on the hair on her legs. Hair that she had specifically grown out in order to repulse her longtime boyfriend who she "couldn't stand any longer." This was Jean. I fucking loved her on sight.

We got on instantly. Her banter was refreshing. She cut right through all my pseudo-charm and bullshit bravado. We laughed. We made fun of each other from the get-go, which to me is a true sign of friendship. True friendship is being able to look your best friends in the eye and make fun of their deepest insecurities, call back the biggest mistakes of their lives, and say things that would normally get you punched in the head without fear of consequence.

That is trust. You can say these things to me because I trust that you don't mean a word of them. If you did, it would utterly destroy me. But you don't. That's why it's fun. It's a safe version of the thing that would decimate me. Friends that don't take banter well do not trust you. They think you mean the horrible things you say and that means that they think, underneath it all, you are horrible. Or

* Please understand, I take no greater pleasure in life than being the cancerous mole. But we'll get on to that later.

that they are. Dump these cunts. They're not fun enough for us.

I broke up with my girlfriend about three months later. Naturally, I lost touch with Jean. We'd occasionally bump into each other at mutual friends' gatherings. Unfortunately, "I used to pump your best mate, then I broke her heart" isn't exactly a strong basis for a relationship. Especially seeing as I had a newer girlfriend who my heart was utterly focused on at the time.

Don't worry, all was not lost. About three years later, after the newer relationship was truly past its use-by date, I was appearing at the Edinburgh Fringe Festival during the month of August. Accommodations were much sought-after. In fact, basically impossible to find. But as chance would have it, my friend Ally and his girlfriend decided they would let me sleep on their living room floor. Their flatmate? You guessed it . . . Betty White.

No, it was Jean.

Now, heads up, I am not going to come across well in this chapter. If it appears that I was a selfish cunt with no respect for anyone other than himself, it's because I was. I'm not proud of a lot of the things I did. But I did them and here we are. All you need to concern yourself with is the fact that now I have Jean's forgiveness and under no circumstance do I need yours. If you'd like an apology from a comedian, then go and find a lesser one.

I won't offer any excuses for my actions. I will give you

some context so that you can understand my naïve perspective, my selfish outlook, and why I thought I did nothing wrong.

During my aforementioned three-year relationship, I had done my first TV gig, my second TV gig, and then third and fourth. I'd done two sold-out runs at the Edinburgh Festival and was making a name for myself. This, along with my incredible girlfriend at the time, helped boost my confidence beyond what it had been in high school, where I was treated like muesli at an all-you-can-eat breakfast bar. Sure, it's probably better for you than most other choices, but it's not exactly filling.

I was somewhat of a Z-list celebrity in Scotland. Still am, thank you very much. Nowadays I can hardly walk down Princes Street in Edinburgh without desperately searching the eyes of strangers walking past me, looking for any hint of recognition beyond "The fuck are you looking at, bawbag?"

This is a roundabout way of me telling you that some women were finally paying a little bit of sexual attention to me. I was no longer seen as "the nice guy"; I was "the semi-famous guy it might be worth getting a ride from." And as you'll soon find out, every nice guy is an absolute piece of shit. It just requires enough confidence and attention to let it bubble to the surface.

I managed to avoid temptation while in the relationship. But as soon as I was single, I cashed in on it. I'd heard all these stories from other comedians about how many people they'd slept with, how filthy it was, how often and regular. It sounded like a dream. A dream I wanted to live. Sound shallow? It is. I don't know what else to tell you. I wanted to be an all-you-can-fuck buffet.

So I did it. I spent that entire festival having as much sex with as many people as I could (safely). It was excellent. One-night stands, two-day stands, fuck buddies, dating, fingering in nightclubs. I was well and truly living the dream.

This isn't the bit I'm ashamed of, by the way. If you're expecting me to look back and regret having fun, consensual sex with multiple partners, none of whom were expecting anything other than sex, then I'm afraid you (much like twenty-one-year-old me) are fucked.

When I wasn't "spurting the gurt"* as often as I could, I was spending the time with Ally and Jean. We were young, student-young, comedian-poor, and living in the center of Edinburgh during the festival. We smoked weed, we drank every night, we threw up in every single back alley in Edinburgh. It was one of the best months of my life.

During this time, I got to know Jean better than I had when I was trying to get her best friend naked. Weird, that. At first it was quite hard getting close to her. She wasn't cold. She also wasn't overly affectionate. I'm a hugger. I love hugs. Spooning is the best. Especially when hungover. It

---

* I'm honestly just trying to find my publisher's line at this point. You poor readers are suffering because of it.

took a while, but Jean became a hugger. With a hard R. I wore her down.

We became close. We'd help each other with the opposite sex when we went out. There's nothing better than having a girl be able to tell you what the subtle looks from other women mean. Who is eyeing you up and what it could mean, how to approach them. I wasn't much help in return. Yeah, that guy who yelled "Show me your tits" probably does fancy you, but I don't think you should shag him. Why? Call it a mother's intuition.

We'd go see comedy shows together, bonding over our incredibly similar senses of humor. We'd share and laugh about our failed conquests while watching *How I Met Your Mother* in reruns (only the first four seasons, naturally).

Inevitably we got drunk and banged. Of course that happened. In what world would that not happen? It wasn't a romantic thing. It was two people of the opposite sex who enjoyed sex and weren't repulsed by each other going, "Aye, why not?" And we did. It was fine. Fine enough to repeat a few times.

It was all fine and dandy. Right up until the night I got the attention of another girl in a nightclub and decided to bring her back to Jean's apartment—where I was staying—to do the deed. Weirdly, Jean seemed to have a problem with this. But that's women for you.

At the time, I thought I had done nothing wrong. Jean knew I was enjoying being single and she was also enjoying being single. She didn't want a relationship and I didn't want a relationship. We had sex. What, that means I can't have sex with other people? What is this, apartheid? Nonsense.

Look, I now know the error of my ways. It wasn't about me sleeping with other women, it was about me not taking any of her thoughts or feelings into consideration. It was me treating her in the same way that I'd treated all the other women during the month. With respect, but as a one-night stand. Shagging them, then bagging them. Pumping, then dumping. Sexing, then exing. Cumming and running. Fisting and then listing all the reasons why we don't belong together.* It was about me being a selfish little cunt.

Jean decided to be an adult and explain how my actions had made her feel and how I should conduct myself in the future with her and all other women unless I wanted to be regarded as a piece of shit by every living person. She pointed out that I was on a very dangerous path, thinking only about myself, letting incredibly low levels of fame get to my head, and for treating people like her as extras in the sitcom that I thought was my life.

I told her she was going down a very dangerous path of being a dumb bitch and to shut up. You know, like adults do. I moved out of the apartment for the remainder of the festival so that I could shag whoever I wanted without being looked at by the judgmental eyes of someone who wanted better from me.

---

* I can't believe my publisher hasn't canceled the contract by this point. The pervert.

At some point I came to my senses. It didn't take long. People who call you on your shit are a valuable commodity. I make sure to surround myself with people who do not give a single fuck about any of my success. Don't get me wrong, they're all incredibly supportive and proud. But to them I'm still just Sloss—the Cunt. Just because I occasionally get recognized or do work on television doesn't mean I'm not the same moron who thought the term *prima donna* was pre-Madonna and was a method of describing a point in time up until he was twenty-two years old.

If it makes you feel any better (because it certainly makes me feel better), since this incident Jean has been a dogshit friend on at least one occasion, so we're well and truly even. She is one of my best friends in the entire world. We live together. She comes to my parents' for Christmas. We have the greatest breakup tradition of all time. If one of us dumps someone or gets dumped, the other person has to drop everything, turn up at the house with two bottles of wine and two tubs of ice cream, watch *Mean Girls,* and tell the other person he or she is a beautiful phoenix.

We've been friends for nine years now. She's helped me grow as a person in a thousand different ways. She helps with some of my stand-up. If I occasionally come across as likable onstage, I can assure you it's because she's made me rephrase things so I don't come across as the cunt I pretend to be, but as the nice person she seems to think I am. She'll read this chapter several times and give me notes on it. She'll try to make me change the bit where I said she's been a dogshit friend, and she can quite frankly fuck off if she thinks that's going to happen. Get your own book, bitch. You know what you did.

I think having friends of the opposite sex is very important. It teaches you a lot. When you're young the only time you can really learn about the opposite sex is by dating them. Which isn't ideal, because it's both of you pretending to be something you're not. It's like studying animal behavior in a zoo. It's not a fair representation of what they are and how dangerous they can be.

A man having a close female friend is kind of like having an emotional mentor. You can talk about the things you would normally shy away from talking about to your male friends. She allows you to explore another part of yourself.

I don't know what it's like to be a woman being friends with men, but I'd imagine it's similar to what Jane Goodall felt: "These things stink of shit and could kill me, but fucking hell, some of them are close to human."

This might sound naïve, I imagine most of what I say does, but I never realized the fear women feel while walking home at night. It had never occurred to me. I'd be at home and Jean would come back in tears talking about how some random guy had just followed her for a bit. I don't follow women home. It had never occurred to me that this was not only something that happened, but something that happened often.

That doesn't make me a bad person for not knowing any of this. How would I know that? The problem is most men don't know what women go through because we don't go through it or do it. It's out of our realm of imagination. That's male logic. "I'm not part of the problem, therefore I must be part of the solution." Binary ignorance.

What seems obvious to women is something a lot of us men just never considered. It's not malicious. It's ignorant as shit, yes. But it doesn't come from an evil place. It absolutely shouldn't have taken me this long to realize a lot of the things I know now. But it did. I'm grateful to all the women in my life who had the patience to explain things to me.

It opens your eyes a bit. It definitely changed the way I approached dating. I saw how some guys treated Jean and how that made her feel. And realized that I was doing the exact same thing to other women. Even though I absolutely understood where the guys were coming from, I saw the aftermath of what they did. How it affected her and made her feel. This caused me to try and be a bit more sensitive when dating. Instead of thinking I was such a fucking legend.

To women, all of this is probably going to sound incredibly stupid and closed-minded. Yeah, you're right. But you don't know a lot of shit guys go through. Ever had a single long strand of hair wrapped around your dick after a blowjob? No. You haven't. It's proper agony. Just a thread of cheese wire wrapped around your johnson like there's a tiny assassin in your pants trying to choke your pecker out. You don't think about that when you suck us off, do you? No. You think only about yourself.

We'll call that even, yeah?

I don't know what I've taught Jean in return. I hope it's good. I hope I've managed to show her that men aren't inherently evil, cruel, and manipulative the way Twitter would have us believe. We're just self-centered Neanderthals who sometimes need direction and don't react well to being yelled at. I hope that living with me and seeing a man in his natural territory when I'm not trying to impress anyone hasn't made her lose too much faith in the world. She's not a lesbian yet, so that's something.

If your best friend is a different gender from you, I strongly recommend you fuck. It's crucial. Not to see if there is any sexual chemistry there; there probably won't be. But curiosity kills. It's better to get the curiosity out of the way at the start of the friendship, realize that it's a terrible decision early on, and then it won't come again for the rest of the friendship. I have drunkenly shared beds with Jean on multiple occasions and neither of us came close to making a move. Why? Because we've done it. We know it's not for us.

You don't really get that curiosity with your friends of the same sex. Maybe you do. I'm heterosexual, so I'm not attracted to any of my guy friends. Don't take that to mean I'm one of those blokes who can't appreciate a good-looking man. I absolutely can. If Idris Elba asked me to marry him, I'd have to say yes and just get past my straightness. You can't let a little thing like sexuality get between you and the perfect man. I think we'd be a great couple. If I ever annoyed him, he'd just put me on the top shelf of something until I calmed down and then I'd nuzzle warmly into his pectorals, which probably smell like oak.

I've gone off topic. Maybe bi and gay people are attracted to their friends. I have no fucking clue. As you have probably realized, I have no fucking clue about most things. I like to think it's one of my most endearing traits. Yet despite pointing that out several times during this book, some people will still take it seriously.

I'm very aware that this book is heteronormative, and that's because I'm a heterosexual. I'm aware that by changing certain words or giving more examples it could be more inclusive, but I dislike commenting or assuming things about people who live a different life than I do. I don't want to say it's the same for homosexuals or bisexuals or trans people or anything else. Or that it's different. I don't fucking know. That's not the life I live, and it's not my right to comment on their behalf.

"Oh, my God. I bet you and Jean will get married!" That's been said by every person who was raised on Disney and *Friends*. If you have a friend who is the opposite sex, you know all too well how often this thread of dialogue occurs. Some people, plain people, will see two friends with different-shaped junk and think, *Oh, my God, they just don't know it yet. It's so adorable. I got married at twenty-two, I think I know.* Honey, no. Love is actually a fair bit more than that.

"But you're so nice to each other." Really? Someone being nice to you all the time is enough of a basis for you to think he or she is your soul mate? Hoo boy. What a sad, bleak life you must have. I'm so sorry for you.

Why don't Jean and I want to get married? Because we're not *in* love. Just because we get on, love each other, and confide in each other doesn't mean I want to spend the rest of my life with her. If Kai had a sex change, I would support him in every single way I could.* I still wouldn't have sex with him, though. I especially wouldn't marry him.

So for the same reason, I'm not going to marry Jean. If I married her, I wouldn't have anyone to complain about my wife to. I'd be fucked.

I understand the logic. Jean is my best friend, and every single loser that gets married says, "My partner is my best friend." Which I know is true. But it's *eventually* true. If you're in a relationship with someone long enough, that person will become your best friend. That's how proximity and familiarity (and Stockholm syndrome) work. Just because I'm Jean's best friend right now doesn't mean I'm the love of her life. That position is held by cheese. Only a fool of a man would think he could replace cheese.

"Won't it be difficult when one of you gets into a romantic relationship with someone else?" Oh, really! You think I'm that immature to see other men as a threat to my friendship? Spot-on. Well observed. It'll be brutal.

---

* While also making the most horrifically offensive jokes.

As a man, introducing your girlfriend to your guy friends is a very simple, albeit sometimes nerve-racking, experience. You know you've got a good one when all the lads start talking about how much better she is than you and how you're an ugly piece of shit, and, oh, my God, why is this ten fucking a four?

I imagine it's a slightly nicer approach from women to women. They've got that "If you hurt her, you'll have me to answer to," which, to me, is always incredibly adorable. You absolutely have the power to end my relationship with your best friend, but after that you aren't much of a threat. I know this because I'm also not much of a threat. Anytime I've said to one of Jean's boyfriends, "You hurt her, you'll have me to answer to," her partner looks at me in the same way that a farmer looks at a new puppy and thinks, *One day I'll probably have to put you down. For the best.*

Introducing a partner to your friend of the opposite sex is infinitely different. Jealousy is an extremely common factor that has come up multiple times for both of us. I had a girlfriend who, after three months of dating, said, "You love Jean more than me." Of course I do, you fucking psycho. If you love me more than your best friend of seven years, then you appear just to be a snake with tits. It's a different type of love, yes, but the fact that you've instantly turned this into a competition tells me a lot about you.

Jealousy is a sign of insecurity and I'll have nothing to do with it. I'll do everything I can to build your confidence in yourself in order to get rid of that insecurity, but it is not my job to make you love yourself. If you ever, under any circumstance, force me into an ultimatum, you are not going to enjoy where my loyalty lies. Not because I don't love you. But because you don't love me. You think you own me and I won't have it.

Jean has experienced the same thing. To her boyfriends I must be a fucking nightmare. I'm another bloke, who lives with their girlfriend, who knows more about their girlfriend than they do, and who has had incredibly average sex with their girlfriend. I'm seen as a threat.

I absolutely love it.

I shouldn't, but I do. I think it's a primal male thing. I'm five-foot-ten on a warm day and have never been in a fight in my life. I've never been threatening. It's a new feeling. A good feeling. It's a powerful feeling. But with great power comes great responsibility.™

It's a power I haven't always handled with grace. Not in a vindictive or spiteful way. Not even in a jealous way. In a fearful way. When your best friend is the same gender as you, it's very easy to accept a partner, because she's not replacing you in any way. I love Kai's wife, Natalie, because she gives Kai something that I could never give him— blowjobs.

When you're best friends with someone of the opposite sex, their partner is going to be the same sex as you. Everything they have to offer you have to offer. With this comes fear. You don't mind the partner giving your friend the things you don't want to offer her. Sex and whatnot.

But you're terrified of losing that closeness you've once had and that you value.

This ongoing "Ross and Rachel" narrative that everyone forces on an intergender friendship can exact its toll. When enough people tell you that you belong together, you become the minority and it can play around in your head. Essentially your loved ones are gaslighting you to fit their fairy tale of your lives because their love lives have become stagnant and tedious. Through you, they want to feel the romance, love, and destiny they no longer feel. At least to the degree you do.

There have been times in my life when I thought I must be wrong. I must be insane. Everyone thinks Jean and I belong together and I must be wrong for not seeing it. To every one of my friends and family who pushed that on me—fuck you. I know you meant well, but, seriously, fuck you. And if you, dear reader, are doing this to someone, I suggest you fucking stop immediately.

Telling people that they should be in love and that they don't understand their own emotions is insanity. You wouldn't look at someone's life and go and tell them that they should be angry, or sad, or happy. That would make you a bag of shit. That isn't your right.

It fucked with my head for years and years. Thinking I was broken. Thinking I was a monster for not seeing in Jean what everyone else saw. How could I be so incapable of love? Everyone else says I should be in love and I'm not. What is wrong with me?

Nothing. Ultimately. If you're in a position similar to the one I've been in, ignore everyone else. You do not owe the world a Disney story. You owe the world nothing other than your best self.

I love Jean. Deeply and profoundly. I would not be the man I am today if not for her. But she is not my soul mate and that's absolutely fine. It doesn't mean she won't be involved in the rest of my life.

I remember a slightly traumatizing conversation I had with my father once. We were sitting in a sauna, as you do, both drunk and talking bollocks. Before I go any further, I'd like to remind you that my father is utterly besotted by my mother to this day. She loves him deeply. But he fucking LOVES her. Always has. Frankly, it's quite pathetic, and slightly daunting, to see how much love a person is capable of, like it could tear him in half if anything happened to it. I'm much like my father, but I don't think I'd be able to handle being that in love so gracefully. The big fucking loser that he is.

He broached the Jean topic and asked if I thought we'd end up together. I said no. But that she'd always be my best friend. He scoffed. "Bollocks." I was slightly taken aback. Not by the words. If you're debating with my father and say something he disagrees with, he'll say the word *bollocks* in the most scathing way you've ever heard. I practice it daily. It's inspirational.

"Why is it bollocks? I'll always be friends with Jean."

"Of course you will. But she won't be your best friend

forever. Or Kai. Or Ally. Or any of the other ones. Every single friend you have is a placeholder until you find the person you're going to marry. Your friends are important. They teach you. They help you. And you should do your best to never lose them. But they don't hold a candle to the love of your life. They are everything and more to you, and if you don't feel that way about them, then you're not in love."

That was terrifying to me. But I can't seem to prove him wrong. I see the love he and my mother have. He has lots of friends. Friends he cares for deeply. But I know for a fact that if you were to ask him to pick between my mother and anyone else in the world, he would be utterly bewildered by the stupidity of your question.

If what he says is true, which I believe it is, then it does mean that in our futures Jean and I will lose a little bit of closeness. I outright refute the possibility that we won't be friends. But realistically she'll meet a man who she wants to marry and I'll meet someone who takes my breath away and they'll become the center of our lives.

As romantic as that sounds, it terrifies the shit out of me. I wouldn't be who I am today if not for Jean. To lose her, even just a piece of her, is daunting and upsetting to a degree I can't put into words.

According to my father, it's worth it.

I hope he's right.

Chapter 5

Countries Are People, Too, Just Bigger and Even Worse

I fucking hate England.

It's one of my favorite places to gig. Some of my fondest memories of being onstage were made in that tea-loving hellhole. Whether it was my first spot at the London Comedy Store, a genuine dream come true for nineteen-year-old me. Or playing at the Latitude Festival and then taking heaps of drugs in a field with my English mates. Or playing the Punch-Drunk gigs in Newcastle, that bearpit of love, kindness, and outright psychos. Some of the best audiences in the world exist in England. It's a source for some of the most interesting history and the home of some of the most beautiful, significant sites.

But I fucking hate England.

I love my English cousins. Every summer we'd all spend a week with my grandparents, having the time of our lives playing in parks and winding up the old folks. Both my goddaughters are English. I love visiting them whenever I'm working down in that Brexit-voting twat crèche. Taking them on long walks through the stunning English countryside, nodding to the friendly locals, chasing my godkids around the park. Pushing them on swings and every time they swing forward and kick me pretending that I get knocked unconscious because I want them to grow up feeling like badasses.

But I fucking HATE England.

Some of my closest friends are English. The lads are from London. Kai is from Blyth, near Newcastle. I was best man at his wedding and he'll be best man at mine. I assume I'll be best man at his second wedding, too. Even perhaps his third. His family and friends are my family and friends. Blyth has become a home away from home for me. I love it there. Don't get me wrong, it's scummy as absolute fucking shit. What a hole. Hideous people, too. Rancid creatures. Proper chores for the eyes.* But the funniest and friendliest pricks I ever did love.

But I FUCKING HATE ENGLAND, MAN!

I'm Scottish. No matter how much I love parts of England, I fucking hate England. Nothing makes me happier than watching those tartan-dodging gammon-shaggers get knocked out of another World Cup and crying because they expected too much. Again. Inject those tears into my veins and I'll live to be 150 years old. It's almost as good as

* I'm just excited for all my Blyth friends to read this, get wound, and text me death threats. Kidding. They can't fucking read.

Scotland winning a World Cup match. I would imagine. The last time Scotland won a World Cup match was two months before I was born.

I was born in England. In Kingston upon Thames on September 11, 1990. (I didn't wish for it. Calm down.)

"THAT MAKES YOU ENGLISH! OH, MY GOD, YOU HYPOCRITE!" (← That's you, that is.)

Well, not really. My mother is from East Kilbride, the city of roundabouts; just outside Glasgow, where both of my grandparents were born and raised. My father is from Thurso, which is the farthest north in Scotland you can go until you get wet.*

My parents met at The University of Edinburgh and were celibate (YES, THEY WERE. SHUT UP) until they both decided to move to England to earn that sweet English money, hoard it, and then return to the motherland. There, once and only once, they fucked. Now, my parents will tell you I am not an accident. I offer to you, the reader, the evidence that has allowed me to arrive at a very different conclusion.

At the time I was conceived my mother didn't have a job and my parents lived on a houseboat in the Thames. As in the fucking river. So either I'm an accident that they grew to accept, love, and raise as if I weren't just a New Year's blowjob that got out of hand (or mouth) OR these

* Yes, Scottish readers. I know John o'Groats technically is, but these morons weren't going to Google that, were they? Nice one. Kids crying.

two psychos looked at their empty bank accounts and their 5x30 floating home that was surrounded by six-foot-deep, needle-ridden piss water and thought, *You know what? I reckon this is the perfect place to raise a child.* Thus making them the worst parents in the history of the world. A stance they ADAMANTLY DEFEND ANY TIME I BRING THIS UP.

At the age of four, when I was just learning to speak fully, I had a cockney accent. A proper little Dick van Dyke chimney-sweep accent. "Oooooo 'Ello, Mumm-ay, 'ello, Dadd-ay. Wot's gone on round 'ere, then?" My Scottish parents were immediately like, "Fuck that. We ain't raising one of those. Get him back north. Across the wall before he starts calling Grandpa 'Guv-na.' It would kill him." So we moved up to East Wemyss, Scotland. Where my actual memories start.

I don't remember any of my time from England. I've heard stories and seen videos. But that might not be me. My parents could be lying. That could be any child they decided to film. All my memories, where my brain came into actual full-blown consciousness, my entire knowledge of myself, come from my time in Scotland. And you think I'm English because I was born there? Eejit.*

If a pregnant woman is on a flight from Edinburgh to Turkey and she gives birth while over Spain, the pilot has

* Scottish for idiot.

as little grasp of geography as I do and probably shouldn't be a pilot. But also, that baby is legally considered Spanish. Scottish mum, Turkish dad (what a diet it's going to have), Spanish passport, having never set foot in Spain. Is that kid Spanish? Fuck no.

I think nationalism is often stupid and used for shitty reasons. If you'd like an example of that, read that last paragraph again. Your mum aimed her fanny at a particular piece of grass within a certain border and you act like not only was it your decision, but it makes you love our country more than me? Get fucked. I have spent 95 percent of my life living in Scotland, but I was born in England so that makes me English? By that logic we're all doctors because we were born in hospitals, anyone born on a highway is a tollbooth operator, anyone born on a plane is a bird, and Jesus was, at best, a chubby little piglet.

You can call me English all you like. My friends all do because they know it riles me. It properly does, too. I really bite. So much so THAT I'M WRITING AN ENTIRE FUCKING CHAPTER ON HOW MUCH I AM NOT ENGLISH. I AM SCOTTISH. I BLEED BLUE AND I SHIT HAGGIS. SHUT UP, KAI. It would be like calling a Canadian an American. Not vice versa. Nobody wants to be American. (Sarcasm, you whiny little Yanks.)

No part of me associates myself with England. I was raised in Fife. I live in Edinburgh. Scotland, to me, always has been and always will be my home. Every time I go to Los Angeles and they say, "When are you moving to America?," I always tell them I'll move to America as soon as they give me so much money that I can buy a private jet and fly home to my real home every fucking weekend. The advance on this book was measly, barely rent money, so I'll be writing it in the rain with no roof over my head.*

I don't hate the English. Scotland hates England. And I'm Scottish, so I hate the English. Make sense? I doubt it.

My English friends still can't fathom the hatred. They don't hate us, they claim. But before the Scottish independence vote (which I'll get into later) England was playing a football match at Wembley where all the fans chanted, "Fuck off, Scotland. Fuck off, Scotland." I know that's not a fair representation of England, and we're as bad as each other, but they fucking started it, Mum.

I don't hate any individual Englishman. Except for Nigel Farage. Who I sincerely hope dies in the next few years.

Understand this—I don't believe anyone has the right to kill another human being. That doesn't mean some people don't deserve to be dead. Some people enter the world and intentionally make it a worse place for the duration of their life. Is it good when these people die? Yes. Of course it is.

But outside of him, I get on with most English people. They're great. Proper funny guys and gals. We share an Isle and they can drink better than the Welsh.

---

* Note to publisher: I'm just joking. I appreciate the opportunity and belief you've shown in me. I'm trying to look cool in front of my new friends. Please still publish this.

The way Scotland hates England is mostly just banter. Don't get me wrong. There are definitely Scots who despise every single English person, as is their birthright. But for a lot of us it's just something we all love to have in common. It's remarkably satisfying to hate the English as a collective, singing, "You can shove your fucking Tories up your arse" (sung to the tune of "She'll Be Coming Round the Mountain"), at every available opportunity. I've also sung that song with Englishmen after England versus Scotland rugby matches. Not football* ones, though. That would be dangerous.

For my American readers, Tory = Conservative. Our Republicans. Less stupid, more evil. And for my Tory readers and Republican readers—HIYA! I don't actually hate you. In fact, I'm impressed you made it this far through my libtard† ramblings. Thanks for having the emotional maturity to understand that despite our differences in politics, we still have more in common with one another than we do with the cunts that we vote for.

Scotland's national anthem is not only easily one of the top five national anthems in the world.‡ It is the only one, that I know of, where the population has added in their

---

* For any American who somehow still doesn't know this, when we say "football," just think "soccer."

† I've always been jealous of the slur *libtard*. The Left doesn't have an equivalent. If we did, it would be *Right-tard,* and that sounds too much like *retard,* and those Right-tards know most of us won't say that word. Well played.

‡ Not you, America. Not even close. If you knew how funny the rest of the world found your little bird song, you'd bomb us all.

own, unofficial, bits in order to directly insult another country. Below is our national anthem. The words in bold are not taught to any of us in school. We all just knew them from birth. It's genetic. Much like they do for the Proclaimers' song "500 Miles," Scottish crowds will naturally divide themselves into two halves each to sing a different, but equally crucial, line of dialogue.

For context, King Edward was a pre-Tory-but-still-definitely-a-fucking-Tory English king that the Scots absolutely battered in the Battle of Stirling Bridge (which also took place on September 11, but in 1297. I spent years loving having that date as a birthday. Not so much now), and despite what *Braveheart* depicts, it actually involved a fucking bridge.

O Flower of Scotland,
When will we see
Your like again,
That fought and died for
Yer wee bit hill and glen
And stood against him. **AGAINST WHO?**
Proud Edward's army! **WANKERS**
And sent him homeward. **WHAT FOR?**
Tae think again.

Kids sing that song. I've seen a seven-year-old argue with his father about whether the insult is "wankers" or "bastards." I fucking love Scotland.

Most of the hate for the English is historic. They're the Auld Enemy. The crumpet-pumping slugs that William Wallace and Robert the Bruce fought for years to try and gain our freedom.

Then, a few years back, we had a vote on freedom. Fifty-five percent of Scotland was like, "Naw, thanks. No *Braveheart* today."

Everyone in Scotland had a different view on the vote before it took place. It was an interesting debate with good points on both sides, despite what both sides will tell you. But we all had the same point of view last year: "Fuck the fucking Tories."

I believe one of the main reasons that Scotland didn't vote for independence is because we quite like being part of Europe and the EU. Always liked it. In fact, before the vote, all the English told us was that if we voted to leave Britain, our EU membership would be revoked, seeing as it was Britain that was in the EU, not Scotland. If Scotland was independent, it would have to reapply and might not get back in. For a lot of Scots that lie swung the decision for them.

The "yes" vote lost by 5 percent.

Two years after that divisive vote took place, more than two-thirds of Scotland voted to stay in Europe. But because we're such a small country with a small population, as always, our vote counted for fuck all. Even if 100 percent of Scots had voted to remain in the EU, it wouldn't have mattered. The English wanted Brexit, so they got it. And they've dragged us out of the EU. They give us a vote in the same way that you fill up an empty beer bottle with water so the kids think they're joining in with the adults.

I believe in democracy. Even though I have many opinions and thoughts on the Brexit vote, which you are fully allowed to disagree with, by the way. I do have my own opinions on how the Brexit debate was carried out, the tensions that were poked at, and the part Rupert Murdoch's cancerous lie-filled tabloids played (can't wait for you to die, either, you old fucking cunt. I hope every second of it is agony. Fuck you, fuck your kids, and fuck your pets). I also don't believe the angle that everyone who voted for Brexit is a racist or had bigoted motives.

Scotland has a population of almost five and a half million. That's less than the population of London, England's capital city. I understand that's why our vote counts for less. But it doesn't just count for less, it counts for fuck all. Sure, we can get MPs in the House of Commons, but in a vote that all of Britain decides, the Scots don't even have to turn up.

There's barely any point to voting as a Scotsman in a general election. Scotland has never voted for the Tories in its history. Yet most of the time the government we have is Tory. For Americans, imagine if no matter how you voted in your election, every time you ended up with a Russian government.

Oh, wait.

So, to my English friends who don't understand why we

continue to hate you and make jokes at your expense, it's because it genuinely doesn't feel like you give a fuck about us. You have power over us. Just because you treat us nicely as individuals doesn't mean that your country doesn't have us right under their thumb. Our opinions don't matter to you as a whole.

Even after the last election where Boris Johnson won by a landslide. Not a single part of Scotland voted for him. We all voted Scottish National Party—the party that is pushing for Scottish independence. We have made our stance very clear. The union has been brilliant. Up until now. Scotland wouldn't be the country it is without your help over the years. Thank you for everything, but let us leave. England is like an overbearing mother refusing to let her child go to university because we're the last child to leave home and she won't know what to do with herself. But we're not the last country; you still have Wales. And Wales actually likes you. The cucks.

Yes, we might fail as an independent country—but I'd rather my country failed on its own. Rather than being dragged in a direction we all fundamentally disagree with.

We tried to leave in order that we could govern ourselves, but your government lied to our pensioners in order to scare them into making a decision that they'd never live to see the consequences of. That's why we celebrate when your shit football team gets knocked out of the World Cup. It's the least you deserve. But I still love you.

Just not as much as I love Scotland, man. It's beyond

stunning. Edinburgh is the most beautiful city on the planet. The history is not only outstanding, but it's revered and protected. My favorite law in the world exists in Edinburgh. No building is allowed to be taller than Edinburgh Castle. Or ever come too near to its height. Edinburgh Castle always has been and always will be the highest point in the city. I think that's wonderful. That's why Edinburgh's skyline is so beautiful. It's not like New York, where buildings are competing for height, stature, and air rights. It's a castle, on a hill, in the middle of some of the oldest streets in the world.

Edinburgh is so beautiful that even doing the walk of shame is stunning. You come out of your consort's student flat, greasy hair, sweaty cock, and breath reeking of fanny.* You walk down cobbled streets that are eight hundred years old. People used to cheer at people getting hanged on these roads. Blood was spilled here. A few witches were probably burned, too (technically, we just burned innocent women, because witches aren't real†). The sun rising over the castle is something that will always make me smile, regardless of how bad my drooth (dry mouth) is.

Probably the best walk of shame in Edinburgh is Grassmarket, a place that's a bit misnamed, seeing as if you smoke weed there, the police officers will tut at you. Not kidding. They tut.

---

* As I've said, *fanny* means vagina in Scotland. In America it means ass. But either way, my statement holds true.

† To every girl from Los Angeles: Witches are not real. You are not a witch. Your friends are not witches. Stop forcing yourself to have an outlandish belief in order to make yourself seem less mundane than you are.

When I first moved to Edinburgh I had this newfound level of freedom. I'd lived at home in Fife until I was twenty-one, pursuing my ill-advised dream of becoming a comedian. All my friends were at uni, and I was sitting across a desk from my mother in her study while she forced me to write jokes because, "If you want it to be your job. You're going to act like it's your fucking job." Now I had my own place, I was an adult! An adult who could do whatever he wanted. Even break the law, as is my right as an adult.

I smoked weed in public. I don't know why marijuana isn't more popular in Scotland. I think it's because it's not a bleak-enough drug. It's very happy. We like whisky and heroin. Sad drugs that keep you miserable. A happy Scotland would freak me the fuck out. I like the dour banter we have. Where we all hate ourselves. (But not as much as we hate the fucking English.)

So I'm walking doon the brae (walking down the street) in Edinburgh, puffing the devil's lettuce. Smoking Hitler's jazz cabbage. Toking on the only green plant a true Scotsman should ever allow to enter his body (salad is for the Tories).

Suddenly, this police officer stands right in front of me. Joint still in my mouth. She looks me dead in the eyes and says, "Do you think you're cool?"

No yelling. No handcuffs. No "Well, well, well, what's going on around here, then?"

Just a cutting question.

I was taken aback. I was like, "No."

She never broke eye contact. "You do."

The worst thing is, she was right. I did think I was cool. That's exactly why I was doing it. It felt cool to break the law. She'd absolutely nailed me. She saw into my soul.

"There's an alleyway, right over there. If you smoked there, I wouldn't have to be having this conversation with you right now. But because you think you're cool, here I am. Not dealing with real crimes, because some wee prick thinks he's Snoop Dogg or whatfuckingever. Don't make me do my job."

"Sorry." I was. I was legitimately sorry. "Don't make me do my job" has got to be one of the most subtle ways of saying, "Could you be less of a fucking cunt, please?," and it's stuck with me. I always hide my drug problem now. Thanks, Police Scotland.

What happened next still makes me laugh to this day. People don't believe it's true. Part of me doesn't believe it's true. I was very high at the time. That affects your memory. That being said, this is how my brain shows me the scenario whenever I recall it.

She took the joint out of my mouth, stamped it on the ground, and then asked, "Do you have any more on you?" I replied that I did not. She just rolled her eyes and said, "Baller." And then fucked off. It was the purest roast I have ever received in my life. I'm still recovering.

Scottish swearing is like no other. It's a true art form; peppering and punctuating your tirade with "fucking," "cunt," "bastard," and "shite" is akin to having a good drummer back up your rant.

When you drive across the border into Scotland from England, we all do a little cheer. It makes me laugh each time. You can see other people doing it in their cars. If you're really excited you can do an "oooooooooooooh" right up until you cross, in the same way we do to put off goalkeepers when they take a goal kick.

When you drive across the border from Scotland to England, you roll down the window and spit. I once did this in a car of Englishmen and was shocked to find they didn't know the tradition. When they did the same going across the border the other way, it felt quite immature. That's our thing, not theirs. But taking other cultures' traditions and making them worse is an English tradition.

Scotland is the only country in the world where Coca-Cola is not the highest-selling drink. Healthy, right? Wrong. It's Irn-Bru. Irn-Bru is the nectar of the gods. It's a fizzy orange drink that tastes like . . . well . . . It tastes like fucking Irn-Bru. It's the ultimate hangover cure. It's laced with sugar and caffeine, and its secret ingredient is iron girders.

Only two people in the world know the secret ingredient to Irn-Bru, which is why America refuses to sell it. Health laws? Fuck that. Irn-Bru wouldn't buckle under the pressure and sell the formula to Coke or Amazon or Disney. I respect that. You can drink it. But you absolutely don't get to know what you're drinking. Stop being such a pussy.

I think Irn-Bru is like a good red wine and needs to be served at room temperature so you can get the most flavor out of it. Heathens will tell you it's better with ice, and they're entitled to their opinion no matter how wrong it is.

Haggis is also absolutely delicious and everyone in Scotland agrees. The reason you think it's disgusting is because we like winding up tourists. One of Scotland's oldest traditions is giving Americans the wrong direction to the castle. It never gets old. Haggis is minced meat with lots of pepper and spices and it's glorious. "Wait! I heard it's sheep guts in intestines." First off, well done for describing a sausage. Moron. That's what *all* sausage is. Ground meat in stomach lining. Only with haggis you don't actually eat the intestines. I've seen Yanks shove asshole-filled hot dogs down their gullets telling me they'll never eat haggis.

Why is haggis a delicacy? For the same reason all delicacies exist. Poverty. The English stole all the good cuts of our meat and left us with the gross cuts. So we ground those cuts up, threw a bunch of spices in to cover up the taste of butthole, and as years have passed we now use the good part of the meat to make it.

Haggis, neeps (turnips), and tatties (potatoes) is our traditional meal, maybe with some whisky sauce if you're in a fancy restaurant. We eat it every Burns Night. Who was Robert Burns? Well, he was a wife-beating alcoholic who wrote some pretty decent poems so we forgave him for the whole . . . you know . . . wife-beating. I strongly recommend you Google Rabbie Burns and read his poems and appreciate how Scottish people can truly be if they put their mind to it. You won't understand a word.

Every Burns Night we whip out the haggis, cook it, and then it's someone's job to recite the "Address to a Haggis," an old Rabbie Burns poem. It can be very beautiful if performed well. Except it usually isn't. Normally it's a drunk granddad just stabbing a big black sausage, while yelling at it in stanzas.

Ever had a full Scottish breakfast? Oh, man. There is nothing like it. Sausage, bacon, eggs, beans, black pudding (haggis with a ton of congealed blood in it), tattie scone (superior Scottish hash brown), and mushrooms and tomatoes for the vegans. It's the diet of every tradesman in Scotland. Down at the bottom of my road in Edinburgh is a diner-type place called the Roseburn Cafe. Greatest full Scottish I've ever had. A small, greasy, cramped place filled with builders throwing coffee down their necks. All of us being served by a truly Scottish staff, "The fuck you wanting? Wae chips? Bru's in the fridge, darling. It'll be right up. Have a seat, sweetheart. DEREK! CUNT'S WANTING A FULL SCOTTISH. AYE, WAE CHIPS." It's my favorite restaurant in the whole world.

A full Scottish is a heart attack on a plate. Australians act all hard because their wildlife is trying to kill them. They're not hard. They open-mouth kiss avocados and can't fathom a breakfast without egg. If you order a coffee in Melbourne, they ask you how you want your egg cooked. Scotland's *food* is trying to kill us. *We're* hard!

At this point I'm assuming you've read all that and thought, *I bet this guy wears a kilt.* You're goddamn right I do. Every celebration. No exceptions. Whether it's a wedding or the funeral of an Englishman. Kilts are great, man. You can pee anywhere. Just lift up the front and boom!

"But what about the underwear?" Oh, honey. A true Scotsman doesn't wear underwear with his kilt. The only time you have to consider it is when you wear a kilt to an English wedding. That's because the English don't normally see people in kilts and will, as is tradition, try and upskirt every Scotsman. They say it's to see if he is indeed a true Scotsman. But I'm certain it's also to check out what a real man's cock looks like.

It's the opposite at Scottish weddings. If you wear underwear with your kilt there, the disdain is palpable. I've seen, and assisted, people chasing down men wearing underwear with their kilts and pantsing them, so that they no longer disparage the memories of their ancestors. No *self-respecting* Scottish woman would dance with a man in a kilt and underwear. The shame she would bring on her tribe would be unbearable. She'd throw herself off the Forth Road Bridge (named because the first three fell down*) and we'd applaud her for it. Don't. Wear. Underwear. With. A. Kilt.

"Doesn't it chafe your cock?" Not if your cock is big enough. So none of us would know.

* It's actually because it crosses the Firth of Forth. But you all believed it, didn't you? HA!

I love Scottish weddings. They're utter carnage. Everyone is shitfaced by about one o'clock. Even the bride. If they're not, it's probably because they're still breastfeeding. So give it an extra hour until that eighth prosecco goes down Mummy's throat, into the tit, and directly in the baby (I don't know how breasts work). Everyone has a hip flask on them, just in case some wank doesn't give out booze at the reception. Someone is always in the corner checking the football scores, complaining about a Saturday-afternoon ceremony, "Fucking pish, man. Nae fucking reception in the Highlands. Hun wedding, this." Then, as is tradition, the bride walks down the aisle. At this point any Scotswoman in the crowd may throw a thistle at her, a symbol that she wishes to challenge the bride for the groom, or sometimes just the dress. It used to be a fight to the death, but with political correctness and whatnot, it's now just until first blood is drawn. Depending on how attractive or rich the groom is, up to ten fights per wedding have been known to happen. And by the end of one fabled wedding, in the confusion of armed combat, blood oaths, and good old-fashioned revenge, the groom ended up marrying his own grandmother.

All right, I made the last bit up. But there was a very famous wedding fight in Aberdeen after the groom sat on the bride's knee and left a skidmark on her white dress. Don't believe me? Fucking Google it. Yeah. Apology accepted.

After the wedding ceremony are the speeches, normally just a roast of the groom and the one joke that must legally be told at every Scottish wedding, under penalty of death:

"I asked the groom if he was going to be wearing a kilt. He said yes. Then I asked, 'What's the tartan?'* and he said, 'Probably a white dress.'" It fucking KILLS.

Then we all get even more shitfaced over dinner. Anyone who doesn't finger a bridesmaid under the table is declared English for the rest of the evening.

Now, what I'm going to tell you next is uniquely Scottish, I believe. It's not going to make much sense to you, but I swear on my very-much-alive mother's grave that every word of this is true, and it happens to every Scottish child, no exception.

For my Scottish readers, if the next section is too upsetting or traumatic for you, I fully understand. Feel free to skip past it. Trigger warning: Scottish country dancing.

Okay, now, to make it clear, I actually enjoy Scottish country dancing. It's incredibly fun at weddings and cèilidhs (pronounced like the name Kayleigh. Kay-Lee. Cèilidhs are a traditional Scottish dance). I am, and every other Scottish person is, more traumatized by the method by which we learn it. It happens in school. During fucking gym class.

---

* *Tart* can mean slut in Scotland. So, "What's the tart in?"

First, you wake up all excited one morning because today you've got gym, which is just an absolute skyve (a class that involves so little work that it's like skipping class). You get to school and your gym teacher, who you watched smoke at lunchtime, tells you how important exercise is. Then he kicks a football into a field and tells you to fuck off. Sometimes he'll change the ball. Rugby, basketball, and one time an actual fucking discus. Even if you're not sporty, gym is still a fun class because you just sit out and do fuck all.

Once you get to school you expect to see everyone else excited. It's gym day, man! The best day of the school week. You look around. Everyone is miserable. No smiles. No gym stuff, either. Why has everyone forgotten their stuff? You see your friend. He's sobbing in a corner. Then it hits you! Scottish country dancing day. Girls are screaming, people are dabbing their faces with red felt-tip pens so they can pretend to have measles, and someone's heard of a promising suicide pact in the chemistry lab. But there's nothing any of us can do. It happens.

We all make our way down to the assembly hall. Sometimes, just out of sheer cruelty, they still make you go into the changing rooms to take off your backpack. In a changing room. To not change. Disgusting. Have you ever walked up a stationary escalator and just felt inexplicably grossed out? In theory it shouldn't feel any different from walking up real stairs, but it absolutely does. It just feels, I don't know, wrong? Well, that's what it's like to go into a fucking changing room and not get changed. The normal joy isn't there. The excitement that this place usually brings has ceased to exist and it's now just a room filled with sad little fully clothed teenagers (I didn't mean to make that last bit sound so Michael Jackson–y, but here we are).

You make your way out to the assembly hall with the same gusto of soldiers who have just been told they're about to go over the top. The girls are on one side. You're on the other.

Then the three little words no pluke-covered (or fake-spot-covered), socially awkward, hormone-ridden teenager ever wants to hear:

"Find a partner."

Those three little words. You have no idea what they do to a brain. It's not that fucking simple. Pick a partner, my arse. There are rules, man. RULES. You can't fly off the blocks like an absolute psycho, can you? The referee blows the whistle and you sprint across to the girl you fancy, IN FRONT OF EVERYONE. Everyone will know you fancy her now. And unless she fancies you, too, you're screwed. And she clearly doesn't, because otherwise why would you have legged it right up to her? You would have both come together naturally in the middle (like those lucky pricks who had boyfriends and girlfriends). Every child who did that sprint is now in jail. I guarantee it.

You can't go too slow off the blocks, either. If you do

that, you might end up with a munter (an absolute minger) (oh, for fuck's sake, that's someone ugly). Look, I know all kids are beautiful to their parents, but most kids are hideous to other kids. We haven't fully developed empathy at that age, so we're cruel. You might end up with the kid that smells. Or worse, you might find out that you're the kid that smells. You can't put your arms around a can of AXE body spray.

Now, I know a lot of my foreign readers will be smugly sitting there thinking you've found a loophole. "Oh, Daniel, why don't you just wait until the very end and hope there is an odd number and you don't get picked?" You go ahead and do that, my son. You do that. I hope you have the fucking time of your life doing the Gay Gordons (genuinely the name of a dance. We know. Shut up) with Miss Stewart the religious studies teacher. See how you live that one down.

For most of us, that was the first time we ever actually spoke to the opposite sex. If you were heterosexual, it was the most awkward thing of your life. If you were homosexual, I imagine it was like being a vegan at a butcher's. And what was the best that could happen? You danced with someone, you made them laugh, they smiled nicely. You both had teeth and, being Scottish, that was a fucking bonus. So your hormones kicked in and you told yourself that you loved this person. Then you had to find her/his mates to get her/his phone number off them. Then you'd have really shite texting for weeks, consisting of old-school emojis and "tb xx" at the end, which meant text back. That's how sexually awkward we all were when we were kids. We assumed that if we didn't tell someone to text back, then they fucking wouldn't.

After all, this person was officially your girlfriend or boyfriend and you were "going out." This meant awkwardly sitting near each other at lunchtime, dancing with the same person at the next Scottish country dancing, and then after school you'd get drunk and finger each other or awkwardly wank each other off in the woods. Young love. Nothing like it.

I'm proud of being Scottish. I'm also realistic about being Scottish. Being Scottish is an important part of who I am. But it's not my defining personality trait. I'd like to think I'm more than the sum of my surroundings. I travel. I experience new cultures. I live in a country where if you fly for an hour in any direction you land in a country that speaks a different language. Or the ocean.

"Oh, you're Scottish? I'm Scottish, too!" says the American, in an American accent, who doesn't own a passport and hasn't left Ohio. No. You're not Scottish. Your heritage is Scottish. You're American. All of your heritage is from Europe, somewhere. Because you're white. That's why you're white Americans. Please. Start reading books that aren't this one.

This chapter might be one that makes me an enemy of some Americans and English. Because they'll take it personally. They'll see the word *English* or *American* and go, "OH . . . That's me! He's insulting me. My personality, my family, my friends, and me."

No. I'm insulting the place where you're from. Grow up.

We insult everything in Scotland. Even ourselves. It's a pessimistic country. I like that a lot. Being a pessimist taught me to appreciate everything good that happened, before the English could come and steal it.

We're a small country, so maybe part of it is Small Country syndrome. Maybe some of my hate toward the English is jealousy. I doubt it. But I guess it's possible. I think a lot of my exaggerated hate comes from the fact that I get told I'm not Scottish by other Scots. Despite my entire family being Scottish, living in Scotland, loving Scotland, paying taxes in Scotland, and writing an entire chapter about how much I love Scotland.

But because I have a Caithness accent (I sound identical to my father) and I enunciate a lot, due to the fact that I perform comedy in countries where English isn't always the first language, I don't sound THAT Scottish. So I try to sound more Scottish by backing the Scottish sentiment of hating the English. Maybe that's where my semi-faux hatred comes in. Maybe I'm alone. No idea. This is a book of opinions, not facts.

I also know that after reading this chapter, 97 percent of my fellow Scots will take to Twitter to make jokes calling me English because I've very foolishly revealed how much it annoys me. I know that. I love that.

But I want you all to know that it'll only help to make me feel more Scottish. As that's what being Scottish is. Giving abuse to anyone and everyone, regardless of race, gender, class, religion, or sexuality. True equality.

That, and I REALLY fucking hate England.

Chapter 6

I Love America, But . . .

America is the greatest country in the world, according to very little evidence and every American I've ever met. It's hard to criticize America. Well, actually, it's not. It's incredibly easy to criticize America. They give you a new reason every single day. What's difficult is criticizing America in front of Americans. They get so sensitive the second you suggest that they might not be the greatest country in the world. You have to preface every criticism with "I love America, but . . ." If you don't put that little caveat in, they see it as an act of war, and we all know how much they love a war. Especially unwinnable wars. The War on Drugs. The War on Terror. Vietnam.

Listen here, Americans, and listen good. I've been visiting your country twice a year, minimum, since I was eight years old. I've been all over. I've stayed in it for three months at a time. I've met a wide range of people, fucked a bunch of you, too. So understand that this isn't coming from a bad place. This is just my experience of you.

I love America. I do. It's absolutely bonkers, but it is

a great country. The best in the world? Not a chance. It's potentially the coolest. Maybe the funnest. The best? Take an absolute running fuck to yourself. Be real. Pregnant women have to pay to give birth. Ambulances charge more than taxis. That's insanity.

In the UK, also not the greatest country in the world, I could literally throw myself in front of a car, go to the hospital, and get fixed up, and the only chance I'll have of losing any money is if the driver decides to rightfully sue me for my dangerous behavior. If someone shoots you in America, you have a bill to pay. Guys, wake the fuck up. That is not greatest-country-in-the-world behavior.

In order to make sure Americans don't throw this book against a wall after reading minor but accurate criticisms of themselves, allow me to tell you all the ways I love thee, America. Then I'll shit on you from a great height.

Most Americans are truly kind people. Every time I've been to a red state, a part of the country where I do not align with the locals politically, religiously, romantically, or even ethically, I have been welcomed with open arms. I've been blown away by the friendliness of the locals. There are definitely plenty of cunts, too. But I find that the people are not filled with genuine hate, just fear and wrong information.

I also obviously have the rose-tinted glasses of being a white boy with a semi-respectable accent. I get the VIP treatment in America, but from my personal and privileged experience, Americans are, on average, the nicest people.

Americans ask you how your day is and then listen to the answer. Like psychopaths. Conversations exist in the UK as performance pieces. You go through conversation for tradition's sake, to come across as polite. Not because you actually give a shit.

"Hi, how are you?"

"I'm good. How are you?"

"Good. Thanks for asking. Busy day?"

"Not too bad."

"Lucky."

"Indeed."

See that? See how no information was exchanged there? Bliss. Those are rehearsed lines that are drilled into your brain as a British child. Never deviate. Never go off script. Even if you're having a miserable day, you keep it to your fucking self. You suffer in goddamn silence. If you ask people in the UK how they're doing and they answer with anything other than "Fine," you are allowed to phone the police and have them arrested.

Americans care. They actually give a shit about how you are and want to do anything to improve your existence. They'll be your counselor, your advice-giver, your sage. I'm happy to overlook their big, dumbass, too-white teeth and their oversized personalities.

I think the reason Americans believe in stereotypes is because stereotypes exist everywhere you turn in America. In Scotland you will never find a ginger man wearing a kilt, playing the bagpipes, drinking whisky, face painted blue, with his awful teeth and heroin needle hanging out of his arm as he punches a woman. All those things exist separately in Scotland, but never once have they coalesced in the body of only one Scotsman.

In Australia, no matter how hard you look, you'll never come across a bloke with corks on his hat, yelling "A dingo ate my baby" at a homosexual at whom he is repeatedly throwing a boomerang. That's a stereotype. That would be absurd.

America has actual cowboys. In New York, I genuinely heard a man yell "Hey! I'm walking here!" at a taxi that nearly ran him over. I promise you there is a man in Florida who wears an American flag shirt every day, has fought an alligator, owns a gun, lives in a trailer, and drinks beer on a porch while being racist. There's at least a hundred of those. I guarantee it.

I have seen people in America who, if I wrote them as characters in a British sitcom, I would be firmly told to "tone down the bigotry" despite the fact that they are portrayed 100 percent accurately. I've seen grown American men cry listening to the national anthem. I've seen women with terrible haircuts demand to speak to the manager. Things that are just memes in the rest of the world not only exist by the hordes in the States, they have Social Security numbers and can vote.

It's because there are more than 300 million of them. It's mental that they consider themselves one country. America is roughly the same size as Europe, which has forty-four countries in it. America has fifty states. Yet all Americans identify as Americans. I'm from Scotland, I live a hundred miles from England. But if you call me English, I will put you through a fucking wall.

The French and the Germans aren't the same. Sweden and Norway aren't the same. Jesus Christ, the Irelands aren't even the same. Even though there is a huge difference between Texas and New York and the people that inhabit them, they all consider themselves American above all else. I don't know whether I admire that or not.

Americans always tell you they're American, too, as if you couldn't work it out from the fact that they smile in a Stepford Wives type way. "I'm an American." Yeah, I got that, Chuck. I got that because I heard you sincerely utter the phrase "Oh my gosh, it's so old," while pointing at a piece of architecture that was built a hundred years ago. None of you are subtle.

I like visiting America, while it's still there. Going to America can feel like visiting the dodos. When Americans ask why tourists take so many photos, I answer, "For future libraries." Then I have to explain what a library is.

I love drinking in America. They don't have restricted alcohol measurements like they do in the UK or those other countries where people dying is considered a negative thing. In a country where you can buy an assault rifle over the counter and that profits off health care, why on earth would they limit how much alcohol you can pickle yourself in?

There isn't a tipping culture in the UK. You can tip.

Most people do. You're a wank if you don't. It's about 10 percent. The employees don't rely on them in the same way Americans do. American bartenders need tips because their minimum wage doesn't cover shit.

Australia's minimum wage is something like forty bucks an hour and that's why they give the worst service in the entire world. Take a seat, America, I'll get back to you. Aussies, you're up, you lazy fucking bastards. Christ, you suck at service. I don't care who you are in Australia, that applies to every single one of you. You suck at service because you're spoiled. You don't need tips to live, so you put an almost French level of effort into hospitality. You don't fear your customers because you don't really need them.

You'll get to them within an hour or two. If you're polite, it's because you're a nice person. You're choosing to be polite. If you're having a shit day, you'll more than happily take it out on my dining experience, as if I'm the reason your dad never hugged you. The great thing about Aussies is I don't even have to end this tirade with "But I still love Aussies" because they won't give a shit. They can take a punch and give it right back. Unlike you bitchy little Yanks. Yes, back to you. In America, servers need tips to live. I don't like this, but it does mean the service is excellent everywhere. That, coupled with most Americans being lovely, means their service staffs are the friendliest on the planet.

I go into a bar. I order my gin and tonic because I have the drinking palate of an eighty-five-year-old widowed woman. The bartender then pours gin into a glass. Not some. Not a bit more than usual. Fucking half. Half gin, half tonic. That's not what a gin and tonic is, you psycho. That's not a drink. That's a commitment.

I'll still drink the drink, obviously. I'm Scottish. I'm thrilled at this turn of events. That's three times the normal measure of gin I'm used to, and it's the same price. So of course I tip heavy. I'll double it. What great service.

That's my first mistake. The bartender looks down at my five-dollar tip and thinks to him- or herself, *Holy shit. Five bucks. I love this guy. I'll keep an eye on this little millionaire.*

I drink my gin and tonic. Like a man. Yes, like a man. All you beer-drinking losers are too macho to admit that beer tastes like a thousand sweaty buttholes. You sit there throwing shade at real men, like me, who down cocktails. You're too fragile and too proud to admit that fruit tastes better than wheat. Drink for drink, I'll floor you. You do a beer, I'll do my pornstar-martini, and I promise you, you'll die. End of you. RIP, bitch.

I'll finish my gin and tonic and order another one. The bartender sees my raised hand, comes down, and goes "Oh, this bloke. The big tipper. Ol' Fish and Tips. Tippy Longstocking. My best friend. I'll give him a bigger measurement, as a thank-you for the big tip."

I then watch this murderer fill the glass three-quarters of the way with gin and then splash in some tonic. I sit there thinking, *Oh, my God. This guy is a legend. That's far too much gin. I'll have to give him another big tip as a thank-you, and then give him a thumbs-up to signal that he's nailed this measurement, and not to deviate from said measurement.* I'll also squeeze ninety limes in there to dilute the taste and stop my scurvy from getting any worse than it already is. I tip another three dollars, so that maybe next time he doesn't pour as much gin.

Then this greedy little man sees the three dollars' worth of tip and thinks, *That's still triple the normal tip amount. I still love this man. I will look after him. He's drinking to forget.* I choke back this 75 percent gin, 15 percent tonic, and 10 percent ice over ten minutes. I'm tipsy. I've basically had eight British gin and tonics. My brain doesn't register the difference. I'm in denial. I can't be drunk after two drinks. If I was, I'd never be allowed back in Scotland. Babies who hadn't even walked yet would spit at me from their strollers. Their first words would be homophobic slurs.

I order my third. The bartender, who would now literally die for me, pours an entire glass of gin. All the way to the top. Plops in some ice and then bends down and whispers the word *tonic* into the glass and hands it to me. I then choke an entire lime into this glass like it owes me money. It's a Sour Patch Kid glass of suicide at this point. Still booze, though, so I'm not turning it down. Never. I tip another five dollars because at this point this guy is running his bar at a loss. I'm tipping to make him stop. Please stop. Just make normal ones. I don't have the strength to say no.

His mind is blown that I've tipped again. I shit you not, this professional will then give me a free drink. I've tipped so much, thirteen dollars, that he now has to buy me one. Whether it's just a free round or whether he pours me a shot and does it with me. As if we're friends. We're not friends. My real friends would never make me drink pure gin. I am scared of this man and I drink through sheer pride and fear. I have now consumed three times my normal consumption of alcohol in four drinks. All for less than fifty dollars. Madness.

I then wake up two days later, wondering why I still give Americans shit when it comes to their drinking culture. I still do, though. You pussies.

I think we don't take Americans' drinking abilities seriously because they consider drinking at nineteen underage drinking. That is hysterical to the rest of the world. Utter madness. Underage drinking at nineteen. HAHAHA-HAHA. That's like saying, "I had underage sex at the innocent age of thirty-one." If you haven't had a drink by nineteen anywhere in Europe, you are a devout Catholic.

Some Americans genuinely don't drink until they're twenty-one. Then they go mental on it. They go from having never tasted alcohol in their lives to college, where they chug beers through a funnel because they don't know their limits. They haven't practiced.

Even though at this point I don't think I've said anything too bad about the States, I'm sure I will have riled up a few readers. Americans don't understand banter. Self-deprecation is an alien concept to them. They're all taught that every one of them is a genius who is going to be president one day. I make fun of myself all the time. Why? Everyone is making fun of me, too—might as well join in. That's what we do in the rest of the world. We make fun of one another. We insult one another and say horrible things that we don't mean. It's *funny* to say something horrible that you don't mean.

After doing jokes in America, where I make fun of myself, I get audience members coming up to tell me that they think I'm great and shouldn't be so hard on myself. It's such a kind thing, but they're missing the point. It would be like going up to a magician and saying, "Look, I'm relieved she's back in one piece, but I really don't think you should be sawing a woman in half in the first place."

Americans don't criticize themselves, so they don't like it when you do it. There are going to be Americans who read this chapter and get really angry about all the things I'm saying, and they won't even realize they're proving my point, that you can find flaws in something and still like it. They've been raised with the ideology that since they are the greatest country in the world, everything in America has to be the greatest, too. It's not American if it's not the best.

"Best Pizza in New York." "Best Coffee in L.A." "World's Greatest Dad." Can you not just be average at shit and accept it? What's wrong with being mediocre? Your mum is fine with it.

I'm never allowed to be 100 percent honest when I discuss what I think about America because some Americans take it so personally that they hate me for the rest of my life. So even though this is my book, I don't think it's appropriate to . . .

Oh, fuck it, let's go for it.

I don't think there is a single normal person in all of America. I've never met one American who I didn't think was putting on an act the entire time we were talking. Everything is so big, so animated. So over the top. Even the introverts will yell in your face about how introverted they are. I don't know whether it's because I grew up watching American television, but I associate that accent with cheesy acting.

Americans are just naturally overactors. Every American is set to eleven every second of every day. Every American is a professional American. This isn't a criticism, it's an observation. I love how my American friends are so animated. Every day is like being in a sitcom.

They're utterly insane. No other breed of people clap when a plane lands. I've never, in my 100+ flights in America, been on a plane where at least 50 percent of the passengers didn't applaud when the machine did the thing it was specifically designed to do and does literally 99.9999 percent of the time.

Once on a flight back from Spain, an American clapped when the plane landed in London and three British people from separate sections of the plane yelled, "No!" at him. Rightfully so. Pathetic behavior.

Americans are simultaneously the kindest people and

the rudest motherfuckers on Earth. They don't mean to be rude and their rudeness often comes from a good place. For example: Nowhere, and I mean nowhere, else in the world does any audience "WOO." I've gigged in more than fifty countries. In forty-nine of those, people know to shut the fucking fuck up when a performer is onstage. They understand that yelling "WOO!" is probably the lowest form of agreement in the world. They're aware that screeching during an oral performance is probably not beneficial to the act onstage and detrimental to the experience of other theatergoers.

I understand that Americans do it because they love and agree with you. They don't know they're fucking up the entire show. They're so happy to see and hear you, they literally can't hold it in. They scream because it's all their tiny minds can process. It comes from the sweetest, kindest place, yet it's still the rudest thing I've ever experienced in my life. Mid-fucking-monologue onstage. Doing a job that relies on timing. Performing routines that require me holding tension in the room only to have some absolute Neanderthal go, "Oh, my God. I agree with the point he's making. Everyone within a mile of me must know I feel the same way. WOO!"

It's hard to get upset about it. It's like yelling at a puppy for pissing on the floor three hours ago. It has no concept of why you're angry at it. It's just devastated that you are. Looking up, being like, "All I did was try to love you. I'm sorry I did it wrong." It makes me feel like an asshole to complain about this.

For any Yanks still reading this diatribe, allow me to present you with a list of places where the rest of the world keeps quiet. Some are going to blow your mind.

The theater: Yeah. Weirdly enough, we tend to realize that the other people in the auditorium paid to see the same show we did. Out of mutual respect, we try not to make them aware of our presence in the hopes that they won't remind us of theirs as we all face the stage and watch the performance.

The cinema: Bonkers. I know. There's a really good tradition in the UK of shutting your goddamn fucking mouth for the entirety of a movie. Even the trailers. I have seen one person talking during a movie in the UK. Nobody said anything to him, as it's not polite to do so, but the looks of hatred he got from the rest of the audience were enough to give that one rude cunt brain cancer. Every movie theater I've been to in America involves listening to a running commentary from almost every member of the audience. Americans have never been shushed before, and it shows. Why watch a movie when you're the main character in your own.

Elevators: America: Do. Not. Talk. To. People. In. Elevators. Jesus fucking Christ. You could be bleeding to death in an elevator in Scotland and no one will make eye contact with you. We'll all face the door and be quiet, as

God intended. The people bleeding to death won't even attempt to talk to you. They know the rules. They'll wait until they're out of the elevator and go find a member of the staff.

That being said, I enjoy talking to Americans. They're just so different from everyone else in the world.

I went to Trump's 2017 inauguration. That surprises a lot of people, but rest assured I only went because I hate Mexicans and I want America to be great again.

I was doing gigs in Washington at a club there, and my friend Eric, who was opening for me, phoned and said, "You know that's the weekend of Trump's inauguration, don't you?" We were so excited. Anything could happen. John F. Anything could happen. It was a huge day for the world.

We went because we wanted to talk to the Trump supporters. The media had assured me that all Trump supporters were God-loving, flag-waving, dumb redneck racists. I tend not to trust the news, like a lot of Trump supporters. Unlike Trump supporters, I think Rupert Murdoch is the most cancerous person that has ever lived. I believe the Murdoch family has done more damage to the human race and society than any other family in history. I believe they are, from their very core, pure evil. If you want to know the biggest cause of polarization in America, look no further than Fox News and its sister outlets.

But I just couldn't wrap my head around every single Trump supporter being a bigot. Some of them would be, sure, that's where the bigots go. But half of the country? I didn't and still don't believe it. I wanted to check for myself. Going to the inauguration was my way of talking to these people and making my own judgment call. It was also a front-row seat if anything crazy went down.

Before I go any further, I want to clarify that I'm not trying to make any political point here. I am obviously not a big fan of Trump's. I, like 95 percent of the non-American population, see him as an unfathomably stupid, cartoonishly evil blob of sentient hate that has a grasp of language similar to a parrot on Adderall that has been drip-fed videos of Alex Jones masturbating directly into his own mouth as his new "cure-all remedy for the COVID-19 hoax." Bashing him to score points in a book you've already bought seems a bit pointless. Yet fun. I don't have anything fresh to say about the man. I went to his inauguration. I was there. Everything I'm about to tell you is true. I don't have an agenda here apart from saying horrible yet accurate things about a people who inherently cannot take criticism simply because I am an attention-seeking twat.

We got straight to the front. Not of the paid bit. Just the bit that was free to enter. No queue. When Trump says it was packed, which, weirdly enough, he is still harping on about, he is lying. I was there. When we saw the photos of Obama's inauguration taken from above, we were gobsmacked. Trump's was a third the size. Maximum. That doesn't mean it wasn't a lot of people. It was just nowhere near his claims. I have seen his lies in action. I was part of one.

There were a lot of Trump supporters and a lot of

anti-Trump protesters. The supporters outnumbered the protesters because most of the protesters were doing their thing in other parts of the city. It would have been counter-intuitive of them to attend the very thing they opposed. Some still did, though.

What surprised me the most was the reaction when the Obamas walked out. I was expecting jeers from this crowd of mostly Republicans. There were a few, but nowhere near what I thought. I'd say maybe 20 percent of the crowd booed. The majority applauded. People in MAGA hats were like, "Respect where respect is due." And they clapped. The Trumps walked out and the booing went up to about 30 to 35 percent. This just made the supporters cheer louder.

Then the camera panned to the Clintons, and I've never heard booing like it in my life. Thankfully. It was deafening. Easily 75 percent of the crowd booing. Jeers and shouts and hisses. It was like being at a Pantomime.* I had no idea why. All I knew about Hillary Clinton is the stuff I saw in the buildup to the election and the fact that her hubby got noshed off by that lady under the table in that office where you probably shouldn't get blowjobs.

We started talking to the Trump supporters. Sorry to disappoint a lot of you: I met some lovely, kind, coherent, intelligent individuals who were more than happy for a spirited yet friendly debate about the new president. That being said, some of them were straight up absolutely the dumbest people I have ever met in my life. Thick as pig

* See page 212.

shit. I can't wrap my head around getting to fifty years old and still being that stupid. It's an outstanding achievement. Genuinely stupider than a lot of children I know.

Eric asked a woman, who was in full American flag and Trump gear, how she felt about Trump's saying, "Grab 'em by the pussy." Which he did say and admits he said. Her reaction was one of disgust. She said, "Do not use that term in front of me. It's disgusting." When Eric pointed out that he was directly quoting the man she supported, she just kept repeating "Do not say that foul word in front of me." That was it. There was no discussion. No reasoning. It was like talking to a toy that was only programmed to say five phrases.

I also saw a black dude selling MAGA hats, and I asked him if he supported Trump. He replied, "Nah, just here to make money off idiots." So I bought a hat off him because I respect the hustle, and I am an idiot. I'm his target demographic.

I also spoke to a very intelligent eighteen-year-old Republican and her mother. They were incredibly polite but firm in their support of Trump. They truly believed he was the better option because they hated Hillary so much. I learned from the inauguration that most people didn't actually fully support Trump. They just utterly hated Hillary Clinton. Venomous hate for the whole family. I'm still not really sure what they've done to deserve such venom. I'm not here to offer an opinion. I'm just trying to give you the least biased account of events that I can, and part of that's to tell you that a lot of Americans absolutely despise the Clintons. That was a bit of a shock to me.

The rest of the Trump supporters were mainly nice. But it was a toxic environment. People were either so pro-Trump or so anti-Trump, and both factions were in close proximity. You felt the contempt in the air. It didn't come only from one side. Both sides hated each other equally, and it was palpable in the air I breathed. It was not the America I had become accustomed to.

That has changed in the past four years. Drastically. Trump played a blinder, riling up the gleefully miseducated masses with lies that they were desperate to believe. That worked wonders on people who were raised Catholic. Shock horror. When you raise a people to believe the words of confident white men without any evidence backing them up, is it any wonder seventy-four million people voted for the cunt-Trumpet?

What astounds me isn't Trump's lies. It's his followers' determination to believe the lies. To willfully ignore evidence that can be corroborated. Early in 2020, both the CIA and the FBI said that Russia was interfering in the American election process. Again. Sowing seeds of chaos and disorder to undermine one of the most powerful democratic countries on earth. They said the Russians were planting misinformation to stoke the growing divide between the left and the right.

One of the lies they came across was the idea that Joe Biden has dementia. The evidence to prove this was a compilation of him succumbing to his stutter, which he has had since birth. (Obviously, mocking the disabled is nothing new to Trump and his kin.) Both the FBI and CIA said that the "Biden has dementia" lie came directly from Russia. Trump said, "No, it didn't."

And seventy-four million Americans believed him over the FBI and CIA. Seventy-four million adults believed that two organizations, each with thousands of employees who signed up to work for those organizations out of a love for their country and a desire to defend it against internal and external threats, faked their investigations and findings. All Trump had to do was go, "No, you." Like an old man blaming a fart on a footstool. And SEVENTY-FOUR MILLION of you went, "Sure, good enough for me!"

At this point I have to give a big shout-out to the Trump supporter who genuinely made me laugh by being an absolute dick. Look, being a dick is obviously wrong, but I sometimes find shithousery hilarious. As much as I hate trolling and don't do it, I'm not going to lie and say I don't find some perverse joy in winding someone up. I'm a sibling. I know how good it feels to get right under someone's skin. If you don't, you're either a liar or a saint. As an adult, however, even though it's fun, you're not supposed to do it.

There was a group of anti-Trump protesters shouting, "Not my president! Not my president!" This Trump protester just stood beside them and offered a running commentary of corrections.

"NOT MY PRESIDENT."

"Yes, he is."

"NOT MY PRESIDENT!"

"I think you'll find he most definitely is."

"NOT MY PRESIDENT!"

"That's actually what this whole event is. If you'd stop shouting and start paying attention, you'd realize that's what this is all about."

"NOT MY PRESIDENT!"

"He is, though."

It was such cuntery. I don't condone what he was doing nor support his beliefs. But it made me laugh. It was petulant and childish, but sometimes that tickles me, especially with that man still in total denial about Biden's being elected.

It was fascinating and terrifying to watch the Trump campaign from outside America. America is still very divided on how good a president Trump was. But no other country in the world has any questions at all about that. I don't think Americans understand that even right-wing people from other countries think Trump was and is a giant dumbass. Even their media. I haven't been to a single country where the general public doesn't consider Donald Trump the biggest laughing stock in the world. Somehow it's only within America itself that a lot of people don't see their ex-president for the cartoonishly evil man he is. It shows you how genuinely powerful the propaganda machine that operates in America is.

There's a stereotypical idea in the rest of the world that Americans are stupid. It's a tough point. Americans were the first people to send someone to the moon. That takes genius. They landed a rover on Mars. That was immensely intelligent. Some, if not most, of the smartest people in the world live and work in America. But they're very, very quiet.

American morons are the loudest motherfuckers in the world. Their stupidity is deafening. It's unfair to call the entire country stupid. But we don't remember mediocrity. We remember extremes. And I must say that the dumbest people I have ever met in my life have all come from America. Stupidity to the nth degree.

Once I was reading a book called *How to Kill Your Friends*. It's a good book. I'd recommend it. I was going through LAX and one of the members of TSA took the book out of my bag and asked, "What is this?"

I was stumped. I've never had to explain the concept of a book before. I'd never needed to. People tend to just know. I stuttered and I was like, "It's a book." He looked at me as if I was the idiot.

"Do you think it's an appropriate book to have in an airport?"

Again, stumped. Within my line of sight I could see a bookstore in the section of the airport he was currently not allowing me to enter. I couldn't grasp what point he was getting at. I just replied, "Aye, it's a good book. I like to read."

He looked me dead in the eyes, and this adult, who can vote and legally have children, said, "It's very threatening."

Oh. My. Fucking. God. His problem was that the book

was called *How to Kill Your Friends*. He sincerely believed that's what the book was about. That it was a guide to how to get away with murder. This guy assumed I'd already read *How to Kill Your Enemies* and it was such a great success, now I'd run out of enemies. Thank God there was a sequel.

He also thought he'd outsmarted me. Not only was he the dumbest human being I have ever had an interaction with, he was so stupid, so delusional, that he thought he'd outsmarted me. He'd caught me red-handed. Surely this would get him a promotion. Catching a murderous criminal just casually reading *How to Literally Do a Murder on an Airplane and Get Away with It*.

I cannot fathom that level of stupidity. A ten-year-old in any other country in the world would understand that if you were to have a book that told you how to literally murder people, you probably wouldn't give it the most obvious title in the world. You'd call it something inconspicuous. Like the Bible or the Qur'an.*

An American once asked me if we had television in Scotland. I pointed out that we invented the thing. His response: "No. It was Edison." Edison, by the way, like most prominent American historical figures, was a bag of shit. Just like Columbus, the man who loved a good ol' genocide and has a day dedicated to him in America.

* Cancel me, bitches. See what happens. Your outrage is the greatest form of free publicity in the world. How do you think Trump became president? He said inflammatory things and you all put it on every single channel for every second of every day and he didn't have to pay a penny. Complain about this book, I beg you.

Thomas Edison stole most of his ideas from Nikola Tesla, a man who believed electricity should be free for all, versus an American who had a better grasp of business than the overly trusting Croat/Serbian. (Croatia and Serbia have a big rivalry about whether Tesla is Croatian or Serbian. His mother was Serbian, but he was born in Croatia. I'm not going to get involved.)

This is a very common thread throughout the teaching of American history. It's edited. Most Americans don't know that Columbus was a mass murderer. They don't know Edison was a thieving, treacherous bag of shit. The truth makes them look bad.

In Germany, they're taught about what Germany did during both World Wars. Including the Holocaust. It must be brutal learning what your ancestors were part of. It's also one of the reasons why Germans are so cool and humble. They're not personally ashamed, because they're not the ones who fucking did it, but they know their country's history.

Americans aren't taught about all the evil shit they've done. In the UK, we aren't really, either. And that's why a lot of us are arrogant assholes, too. We still paint ourselves as heroes a lot of the time. Thanks to the inherent evilness of the Nazis, they managed to draw a lot of attention away from how shitty our empire used to be. We used to own a third of the world, and I assure you, we did not pay for it or keep the receipts.

If any European or Brit makes any decent but damning

point about America and/or its history, Americans will happily remind you that if it wasn't for them we'd have lost the war. There's nothing more cutting than hearing "If it wasn't for us, you'd be speaking German" by a fat moron who speaks outrageously bad English.

Americans never see the irony in that. They'll tell English people that it's because of them that they're speaking English. In English. With a straight face.

Again, I LOVE AMERICA. I do. It isn't perfect. Not by a long shot. You have truly done some of the greatest things in history. You have produced some of the finest human beings of all time. Your achievements do not erase your shithousery. It's a balance thing. If you want to boast about how great your country can be, good. Do that. I'm not trying to take that away from you. In return, you have to accept the criticisms that practically everyone else in the world justifiably gives you.

It's not malicious for us to want you to be the best. We want you to be the greatest country in the world because you're the biggest threat to the world. If you continue to sit there with your fingers in your ears singing, "LA LA LA LA LA, why don't you go back home if you don't like it over here?," you're only going to alienate the rest of the world more than you already have.

I don't want that for you. I want the rest of the world to love you as much as I do, but you're making it very difficult for me. So please, for my sake: Get. Your. Shit. Together. America.

Biden's victory was a relief for the rest of the world, but only a brief one. Trump wasn't the problem. He was a symptom of the cancer that exists deep within America. A willfully uneducated population combined with deep-rooted race problems, fear of the outside world, and an inability to accept criticism, means that the next Trump is going to be worse. I don't know what the cure is. I don't know how to fix America. Happily, that's not my job. My job is to make fun of it all and puncture the hypocrisy. Yeah, I know the mantra is "We all must join together, jerk each other off, and heal as a nation," but how do you heal something that was never truly together? How do you fix something that won't admit it's broken? How do you stop the most powerful nation in the world from tearing itself apart from the inside because they've become so scared that they now wish death on their fellow Americans? I don't know. But they sound like questions that the Greatest Country in the World would know the answers to. So start fucking acting like it.

Chapter 7

Lads, Lads, Lads

I can't imagine girls punching one another in the pussy. Well, I can imagine it. Obviously. I'm not mind-blind. I just mean that I'm not even sure they do it. I don't think there has ever been a slumber party where the highlight of the evening was when Claire opened the door and accidentally smashed Jennifer in the fanny with the door handle. All the other girls yelling shit like, "HA! That's the first knob you've had in a while." I'd be genuinely surprised to find out that teenage girls spend a lot of their time trying to work out the funniest way to twat-slap their sisters. I bet I've come up with more creative hymen-Hadoukens than most women.

Even when girls do get hit in the chud* I don't imagine they find it funny. I'd assume that if and when it happens, all the other girls around them are very sympathetic. I

---

* Some of you might accuse me of using these opening few paragraphs to show off my vast collection of euphemisms for lady bagels. How dare you. I'll remind you that I am a published author, thank you very much.

can almost guarantee none of them laughed so hard they vomited.

For a man, there are few things funnier than another man being hit in the testicles. As a comedian who spends his entire career trying to find new, creative, intelligent ways to make people laugh, I know that nothing I ever create will be as naturally funny as seeing someone hit in the balls. Or farts. You can't beat the classics. If a man gets hit in the balls so hard that he farts? I think I'd die of sheer joy on the spot.

Some historians believe that the first-ever laughs came from seeing someone being hurt. Early man achieved consciousness, then became self-aware enough to watch some people injure themselves doing something, understand that it wasn't what they had intended to do, and then laugh at the mistake that was made and the consequences thereafter. So before you accuse me of being childish for laughing at this sort of thing, understand it's literally biological.

Maybe women do find cunt punts funny, and they just hide it better. But I don't think that women have the innate sense of justice to clam slams that boys do to nut shots. If someone hits you in the balls, you get to hit them in the balls back. At any time. It's an IOU for life and no one will complain. I'd die for my friends. But if one of them hits my worst enemy in the balls, then my worst enemy gets to hit my best friend in the nuts and there isn't much I can do about that. Except film it.

You will struggle to find a man who doesn't have this intrinsic sense of cojones karma. If you were to hit the

Dalai Lama right in his dangle berries, I promise you he'll be like, "Aye, namaste and whatnot, but now I have to hit you back. An eye for an eye makes the world go blind, but you flicked it as well, too, and you know that's way worse."

I'm sure there are women out there who do find it a bit funny when a friend gets hurt. As I'm sure there are some men out there who think nut shots are childish. But what the fuck is wrong with that? Being an adult is fucking exhausting. Is it wrong to have brief respites in life when we're nothing more than glorified apes?

Society is going through a very interesting phase right now. On one side you have people who say that gender is a construct and that gender stereotypes are degrading to women and men alike and contribute to the patriarchy's way of keeping women down. On the other side you have traditionalists bemoaning woke culture, identity politics, and "political correctness gone mad." Then you have the rest of us, leaning slightly one way or another from the middle, who don't really give a shit.

But I'm not one of them. I tend to keep my opinions out of the whole gender-identity thing. I identify as a bloke and I've got a big ol' dick. I don't know what it's like not to feel comfortable in your own body, so asking me for my opinion on gender fluidity would be like asking the Pope for his stance on rimming—I've got one, but it doesn't really matter. Sound cowardly? It is. I've seen too many good men and women die in that minefield and I'm not being paid enough to walk through it with a blindfold on.

Even though I have lots of female friends I've always had a very big group of guy friends. Women can absolutely do anything men can do; most of the time they just don't want to. I could talk to Jean about how many wanks* I had the day before, I just wouldn't. She doesn't need to know that, nor does she care. But Barry will be impressed. We'll compare notes. Like true friends.

My first-ever best friend was a kid called Craig. Don't worry. I was a child, too, at this point. This isn't that kind of book. Going to school in Scotland is slightly different from going to school in America, in that you don't stand a chance of getting shot in the fucking head. Which is nice. The commute can be a nightmare, though, so 1–1.

It was second grade, I was seven, when Craig and I first became friends. One week our teacher explained that Craig wouldn't be in class for a while because he'd broken his leg. We immediately started theorizing on how it had happened. Had we shut up and listened to the explanation, then we might have known. But we were too busy passing around theories of him being thrown out of moving cars or falling off cliffs to be reasonable. Our class was essentially the first-ever Twitter.

Craig came back to school and he was an instant celebrity. Nothing interesting ever happened in East Wemyss.

* Do you Americans really need the definition of *wank*? I've lost even more respect for you. But I'm afraid of my editor. So *wank* is a euphemism for "jerking off," "strangling the baby," or the more Scottish "ripping the heid (head) aff (off) it."

Apart from that kid who got murdered in the toilets a hundred years ago (with a knife—au naturel, Americans. Calm the fuck down). So when Craig returned from the hospital in a cast it was like the Second Coming of Christ except that we were all white. That's the only dissimilarity. No further questions.

I wanted to sign that cast so fucking bad, man. There's something about signing a cast that is inexplicably fun. Vandalizing another person's injury: Brilliant. I'd sign my manager's titty-cancer scar if she wasn't such a prude about it. I'd sign my own baby on the way out if I didn't think my future wife would break my fingers. Feel free to sign my coffin.*

Craig's celebrity status quickly wilted. At playtime (recess for you Yanks), his cast meant he could not play football (again: soccer, you dumb bums), thus making him useless. Being good at football is basically the secret to popularity in every single school across Scotland. Whoever is best at football is king of the school. The people's champion. You may be surprised to find out that back in those days it was me. People may be quick to point out that I went to a school that had eighty pupils in the whole place, so being the best wasn't actually that much of an achievement. You ignore those jealous fucks.

Nobody played with Craig, since he was a cripple. It wasn't malicious. Kids just don't really know how to play

---

* Note: I wish to be cremated and thrown into the face of my enemies.

games that don't involve running around all the time. Unless, you guessed it, they have a disabled sister who couldn't run anyway. I was used to playing with people whose legs were shite. So I went straight over to Craig and started playing a game where he threw the ball and I'd run around and then bring it back. The educated among you might realize that this is essentially "fetch," where I'm the dog, and to you I say, "Woof woof, motherfucker. Woof woof." It worked. Craig and I hit it off. I officially was someone's best friend.

For the next six years we were inseparable. Sat beside each other in class, walked to school together, had sleepovers on weekends. We grew up in coastal Scotland, so we used to just explore, play, and beat the shit out of each other.

At one point we were down at the beach. Not your lovely white-sand, sun-in-the-sky, lady-sunbathing-with-a-bit-of-side-boob beach. A Scottish beach. No sand. Just gravel, empty beer cans, and sadness. It was a really stormy day and we wanted to see if the waves were powerful enough to knock us off.

They were.

I say "us," but I meant Craig. I turned around and he was nowhere to be seen.

I remember looking for him in the water, frantically scanning the foamy waves to see if I could see any sign of his terrified face. Every now and then his head would pop up, gasping for air, before being immediately thrown back under the weight of the crashing ocean. There was nothing

I could do. I was helpless. He was helpless. I just sat there watching him go under and resurface and go under yet again. Waiting for the moment that he wouldn't resurface.

Then he stood up.

The water was only up to his waist. So we ran down to the pier again because neither of us had been traumatized enough to learn a lesson. I guess you could say that I . . . gave in to . . . PIER PRESSURE.

No, *you* fuck off.

Craig and I were the bestest friends the world had ever seen. Best friends for life. Forever and ever and ever. No matter what. Until we were ten. Then I ended up going to a different school because the one he went to had an incident where a pupil threw a teacher out the window, so my mum was like, "Maybe we'll send him somewhere else. Somewhere where the teachers aren't weak."

I have no idea where Craig is now. Last I heard he had four kids. But we completely lost touch. I don't even remember being sad about it. I'd made other friends. You just kind of drift apart sometimes.

Your first friends are important because they teach you about friendship, loyalty, and banter. But the second you get the chance to upgrade, you do. The Nokia 3310 was a great phone for its time, but I'm not going to have it until the day I die just because of nostalgia. What am I, the phone version of those vinyl nerds?

In the first couple of years of your life you don't really get to pick your friends. You're assigned to them. School is essentially, "Here's a bunch of kids whose parents fucked the same year that your parents did. Now find something else you have in common." It's a lottery. Sometimes you win, sometimes you lose. Sometimes you think you won the jackpot, then end up going to a bigger school where you realize that you were previously in a bargain-bin raffle.

I've always hated relationships that exist due to proximity. Interactions that are based on vicinity are the lowest form of society. People in elevators with you, neighbors, people you've just had sex with. I can't stand taxi drivers that talk. I'd pay double for there to be a "Do not utter a fucking word to me" option. I talk for a living. I have more than enough friends. I feel secure in my own head and I am comfortable in silence. I hate being held hostage due to social etiquette—talking to someone I'm never going to see again. Shall I invite the pizza delivery guy in for a slice, too? Or should I just return to being a background character in his life?

That's why friendships that last a long period of time are quite special. You both grow and change over the years but somehow don't outgrow each other. These types of friendships are hard to keep going, because once you stop going to school together, you get different jobs or live in entirely separate parts of the country. Friendships shouldn't really take that much effort. They should be effortless most of the time. Life is stressful enough as it is.

I've been mates with Ally since we were twelve years old. We fucking hated each other when we first met. I can't remember why, but it's safe to assume it was my fault. I don't know if you've picked this up yet, but I can be quite abrasive and unpleasant when I want to be. Which is all of the time. I'm not good on a first, second, or even third impression. You really have to get used to me.

I was the cool kid at a school of eighty, and now I was the new kid in a school of nine hundred. I hated it. The "cool" kids didn't reject me, because I didn't even go near them. I was too fucking scared. I felt like a chimpanzee that had been raised in captivity with nice trainers who spoon-fed me bananas, being reintroduced to a colony of wild apes that threw shit at one another, which really isn't a bad description of the Scottish school system in general.

Fortunately, the most accommodating, if terrified, social group is that of the nerd. Everything and everyone is their natural predator, so they cluster together in groups and can be standoffish to almost anyone who approaches them. Thankfully, my father is a giant dweeb, so I'm fluent in Geek, and I was graciously accepted and looked after by these weird little people. Little Ally was one. Big Ali was another. They were called that because, unsurprisingly, one was taller than the other. Now they're both the same height, but the nicknames have stuck and it can be very confusing for some people. One time someone asked if they were brothers. As if they had parents who were the least imaginative morons ever. Guess which country that person was from. Correct.

Nicknames are amazing like that. Scottish kids are absolutely brutal with them. Off the top of my head, here are some of the ones from my school and the reasoning behind them.

Bean: looked like a kidney bean
Fog: was loud and lost his dad at sea
Beevs: had massive front teeth and was a cunt
Tharah: Sarah, who had a lisp
Yank: the American
Fat Jonathon: There was no other Jonathon

I had the nickname New Shoes for about six months because one day, you guessed it, I had new shoes on. Over the course of those six months, plenty of other students bought new shoes, but the mantle was already held by yours truly, so they had to settle for other clever pseudonyms such as Blue-Bagged Cunt and Ginger Prick.

I wasn't great at nicknames, either. I had a friend called Alex at school. He was from Turkey, so he naturally became known as Turkey. We were eleven years old and not creative in any way. But we got in trouble for it because one or two kids who didn't like Alex called him Turkey in a really derogatory way, as opposed to the rest of us, who just called him that because we were idiots and it had stuck.

I remember teachers sitting us down and explaining the concept of racism to us, despite the fact that we were well aware of racism. We'd been to football matches. We'd heard all the racist jokes. They told us that calling him Turkey was racist, which I still don't think it is. Ignorant, yes. In hindsight. For us, him being Turkish made him stand out in our little group of friends. It was no different from referring to Big Ali and Little Ally. For him, it was the thing that made him stand out in school and Scotland. We were bringing it up every single time we mentioned his name. It's only after years of traveling and self-reflection that I realize now the point the teachers were trying to make.

I still don't think it was racist, though. It's only racist if you shout it with enough venom. I had a boss from South Africa whose nickname was Africa, and I didn't think that was racist, either (he was white, put down your fucking blog).

Then again, I'm a honky, so maybe it's not my place to tell people what is and isn't racist.

I've kept most of these friends and I'm incredibly grateful for it. I don't see the Allys as much as I'd like to because I travel for work so much, but when I do it's great. Some friends are able to just transport you back to an easier time. You regress into a younger version of yourself and it's a joyous little nostalgia trip.

Whenever we can, they come over to my place and we play Xbox until the early hours of the morning and sometimes even sleep in the same bedroom like we did when we were kids. Four or five grown men, with mortgages and significant others (who are very patient and understanding about our utter idiocy), keeping one another awake at four in the morning farting and laughing, nipping and punching one another. Morons. I love them.

It's nice to still get to be a kid sometimes, because most of the time you have to act like an adult. That's the one true secret to being an adult: I don't think any of us truly *are* adults. We're just kids who grew up. You do an impression of your mum and dad for long enough and eventually it becomes second nature. I still get giddy when they serve me alcohol legally. I can't believe I'm getting away with it.

Adulthood can be overwhelming, and I say that as someone who doesn't even do the adulthood thing all that much. Some of you are out there working proper, real jobs. Paying bills, making breakfast for your kids, and taking the garbage out. Actual adults. If you do it long enough, you forget what it's like to be a kid and you can potentially lose that part of yourself entirely. I've just realized I'm essentially discussing the plot of *Hook*. What a moron.

Plagiarism of one of the greatest movies of all time aside, I think people who don't have friends from when they are young don't have that anchor to their youth. If you fall into that category, I hope you've found it in other places. Otherwise you're permanently an adult and that sucks. Mind you, all my male friends I met as adults still make me act like a child all the time, so maybe men really are just idiots.

I genuinely love male camaraderie. I know there's all this stuff about toxic masculinity and the dangers of it. I agree with some of it, but it's all a bit too black-and-white for me. Too right-and-wrong. It's all "Men should be allowed to show emotions and understand that asking for help isn't weakness" or "Why doesn't everyone just man up and pull up their boots." Most men I know have found the happy medium.

I bully the living shit out of my friends. They return the favor. When one friend's gran died, our other friends and I spent roughly five hours making memes and videos about his dead gran. One of us even went as far as to make a little video of five Irish men singing a song about how much they had enjoyed fucking his gran while she was still alive and once after she was dead. Did this help the grieving process? Of course it fucking did. Do you know why? Because, in private, we all messaged him separately saying we hoped he was doing okay and if he ever needed to talk, we were there. Horrible to one another publicly, nice to one another privately. That's true friendship.

Men aren't these emotionally stunted Neanderthals that some of society claims we are. Sure, sometimes we are not as good at expressing ourselves emotionally. I agree that in general we need to spend more time and effort checking in to the mental health of men. That being said, don't act as if sitting around drinking barbaric amounts of alcohol and having dick-measuring competitions means that we don't have the empathetic capacity to understand when one of us is struggling.

I've already mentioned one of my best friends in the whole wide world, a man called Kai. He's a comedian, we've toured together for eight years, we lived together for five years, we've done cocaine off of each other, I was best man at his wedding, and I'm sure he'll be best man at my first wedding when I've stolen his wife, who is far too good for him, away from him. Hi, Natalie. See you soon.

Kai and I spend every hour of every day in each other's company for up to five months of the year as we tour around the world together. Despite this, we never really fall out. We yell at each other during arguments and call each other every single name under the sun, but we consider all that a heated debate more than anything else. Falling out is for children; insults are for mature adults.

Guy friends are like brothers, which is why dudes call each other "bro." The Allys are like brothers who are my age. Kai is like a scummy older brother. As if my mum had gone through a rough patch, had Kai, then went, "Holy shit, I need to get my act together." And then shagged my dad and peaked by having me.

I absolutely abuse the privilege of having an older brother, seeing as I never had a real one. Kai is hard as nails. One of the toughest people I know. I, on the other hand, have never been in a fight in my life. I was given a Glasgow kiss once (headbutted), but that's about it. A drunk man once called me a faggot, so I, equally drunk, lectured him on homophobia while simultaneously destroying every single part of his outward appearance. He stuck the nut in,* I went down, and by the time I'd gotten back up, Kai had knocked seven of his teeth out.

Once Kai and I were in a car, on tour, and I was driving. We stopped at a red light, it turned amber, and I didn't move IMMEDIATELY. Naturally, this pissed off the man behind us, who tooted his horn to his small cock's content. I rolled down the window and showed him my bird collection. I have only one, but it had been inside of his mother, so I thought they should be acquainted.

Upon seeing my raised finger, he proceeded to get out of his car. I watched this happen in the rearview mirror and realized immediately that I had bitten off more than I could chew. I turned to Kai to let him know I'd made a terrible mistake, but he was no longer there.

Here's something you should know about Kai. He's been in so many fights (never started one, always finished them, though) that he has broken a lot of watches. So now, before a fight, he takes his watch off. Sensible, if anything. He also takes it off before he masturbates. The first few seconds when he takes his watch off are very exciting.

So when I turn around, Kai isn't there but his watch is. It was just spinning in the air like in the Looney Tunes cartoons.†

Kai got out of the car, looked this man dead in the eyes,

* Headbutted

† I feel I didn't need to specify "cartoons" there. But had I not, I would have sounded like that gran who gets youth culture slightly off: "Oh, I heard ya watch the Looney Tunes and play on your Playbox 360."

and said, "Get back in your car before I fucking steal it." The man immediately reassessed his situation, and through the very same rearview mirror in which I prophesized my own death, I watched a grown man get back into his car, put his seat belt on, lock the car doors, and roll up his car window. Justice. Ish.

Kai knows me better than most people. That being said, I still keep parts of myself hidden from him. Not because I'm ashamed of them, but because I let those parts out to other people, like Jean. People who are better suited to listen to my complaints, my fears, and my insecurities.

I was dating a girl for a while a couple years back and I remember realizing the relationship was coming to a close. Something was missing between us, the spark wasn't there, and, long story short, I ended up getting a blowjob from my dentist. It was her turn to say "Ahhh." I felt like utter, utter shit. And that's because I *was* an utter, utter shit.

Quick side note—this is a moment in the book when I'm going to become unredeemable to some people. Cheating is the biggest no-no in the world to people who've been cheated on. To normal people it's just something that is morally wrong. Despite the fact that I've suggested murder a few times in this book, spoken about drug abuse, and made fun of the dead, this will still be the line in the sand for some people. Kai made the excellent observation that certain women will watch *Dexter* (the TV show) about a serial killer. A man who captures, tortures, and murders people. They will watch this show and when it gets to the point where Dexter cheats on his girlfriend, some women will go, "Oh, my God. I hate him." If that's you—good luck on getting back the money you paid for this book.

Look, some people cheat and some people don't. Those who don't cheat are better people than me, but their loyalty means less. Sure, they might not cheat on you. But they wouldn't cheat on *anyone*. It's a blanket rule. It turns out that I am, disappointingly, capable of cheating. So if I don't cheat on you, then you must be pretty special.

"Once a cheater, always a cheater" is often yelled by people who not only don't believe in human growth, but are also incapable of it themselves. I'm sure they also say things like, "Once a baby, always a baby," because it's true for them. They remain stubborn, petulant little crybabies who decide to project that onto the world. If they took a second to stop, self-reflect, and realize that their inability to learn from mistakes and grow as a human being is ridiculous and annoying, they'd realize that this uncompromising stubbornness and vindictive labeling of others is probably the reason they keep getting cheated on.*

Do I regret cheating? Sure. Ish. I regret it in the sense that I know it was a bad thing to do and I wouldn't particularly enjoy it if it happened to me. But cheating on her made me realize that she wasn't the one for me. You just wouldn't do that to someone with whom you want to spend your entire life. My own cuntery made me realize that she absolutely

* HAHAHAHAHAHAHAHAHAHAHA

deserved better than me. So I broke up with her and she's now in an incredibly happy relationship with a man much better than I. I'm also happier. I regret the act but not the consequences.

Did I tell her I cheated on her? Did I fuck! Absolutely not. I'm not going to do that to someone. She doesn't need that insecurity or lack of trust for the rest of her life. I know it had nothing to do with her. It had to do with me being young and drunk, and fancying my sexy dentist. I was an asshole, in a not-so-great place, and there was nothing she could have done about it. Why would I scar her like that?

Anyway, I did the right thing and broke up with her. She took it well enough. It destroyed me. Breakups are the worst thing in the world. They just suck. There's no good time to do it. There's no perfect way to do it. It's emotionally draining and a horrendous thing to go through. Plus, I felt horrifically guilty. I can make jokes about cheating now, but at the time I felt like the scumbag I absolutely was. I cried. She cried. I left the house and I couldn't drive my car because I was just a puddle of guilt and shame and self-loathing.

I remember sitting in the car and thinking that I was the worst human being that had ever lived. Hitler had nothing on me. What's a little genocide compared to crushing someone's heart? I phoned Jean and she wasn't in the country. It broke her heart. We have our little breakup tradition. The *Mean Girls* and ice-cream one. But all she could do was sit listening to me sob uncontrollably in a car, knowing there was nothing she could do to make me feel better.

I didn't even want to drive home. Kai was there. I didn't want him to see me like this. Kai makes fun of me for things of way less importance than crying. If he saw me bawling, it would be the end of my life. He'd never drop it. I'd never live it down. I couldn't handle the thought of him ripping me into shreds, and then going into the WhatsApp group with the other boys, making fun of me for crying over a little thing like heartbreak.

I sat in the driveway of my house just trying to get my eyes to stop being red and puffy. Then I'd think about how my now-ex would be feeling, because of me, and it drove me to bubble all over again. I changed tack. Kai would be downstairs, in the basement, playing Grand Theft Auto. I could open the door quietly, run to the bathroom, get in the shower, and have one of them sitty-down showers like in *Casino Royale.* That was the plan.

I opened the front door and Kai was right fucking there. If I remember correctly, he was about to go for a run. He looked up to see a mess. I can't even imagine what I looked like. I'm not one of those graceful criers. You know, that single tear rolling down the face of a widow holding on to her two young boys as they watch their father's body being lowered into the ground? Yeah. None of that. I cry like a fat kid who grazed his knee running for the ice-cream truck that he just missed. I look like every bee in the world decided to fuck my eyes in the ass to death. I was genuinely close to calling for my mum at one point.

I stood in the doorway as vulnerable as I've ever been. I knew the barrage of abuse I was about to get, so I closed my eyes and just waited for it. I was then gripped in one of the warmest hugs I've ever felt in my life. No insults. No "What's wrong?" Nothing. He didn't need to know. He just saw his best friend cry and he let me cry. I sobbed into his shoulder for what felt like seven years. I let go, went and had my shower. I sorted myself, and when I came out, he was no longer in his running gear. We sat in the living room with a joint and he handed me the controller to the PlayStation.

We spoke about it a bit. Then we spoke about other stuff. Then he made me laugh. Then I made him laugh. Then we were just two best friends playing computer games together and I felt a lot better. A couple days passed and I was eventually back to my normal self.

Then he fucking destroyed me. Holy shit. Merciless bullying. Nonstop. Impressions of me crying, telling the boys about my tears, anytime something even remotely sad happened running to me with tissues and consoling me. The works.

I love that shit, man. I really do. I love that Jean will let me be emotional and not make me feel bad about that stuff—she'll let that side of me exist freely and nurture it. But I also love the fact that when I'm with the lads I'm expected to be a lad. We're filled with testosterone and we need to get it out. Just because we're giant idiots doesn't mean we're emotionally stunted. I'm reminded of that constantly and I think the rest of the world doesn't understand that.

In public we're filled with bravado and ego. People assume that's what we're like behind closed doors, and some of the time we are. Just because we choose to have our emotional moments in private does not mean they do not exist and it does not mean we are incapable of them. We're big, dumb men, but that doesn't mean we don't have a moral compass and know right from wrong.

A couple years ago, one of the men in our group sexually assaulted a close female friend of mine. We know he did it because we got him to admit it. He had been one of our close friends for eight years. It was beyond awful.

The anger we felt was all-consuming. We felt shame at being friends with someone who was capable of doing that. We were embarrassed that we didn't see it coming. There was a sense of failure for not being able to do anything to help our woman friend. We had failed as human beings. He was our friend and he was a rapist. We're still ashamed of ourselves. It's a huge black spot on our names.

Once we found out what happened we immediately cut him out of our lives. We told him we never wanted to see him again. We made sure that we did everything our survivor friend wanted us to do. However she decided she wanted us to react was how we'd react. If she wanted us to testify, we'd testify. If she wanted him dead, we'd have it arranged. Since then, we've done everything we can to make sure that he won't do it again and that everyone knows what he did and that we no longer have his back.

I still feel horrible about the whole thing. I'm still embarrassed and ashamed of myself. Another case of my ongoing inability to protect the women I love (Oh, hello, toxic masculinity. Lovely to see you again. Have a seat). I've never questioned my morals or my sensibilities more. Did we encourage this? Did our banter and our "lad attitude" give him the sense that we wouldn't care about this? Did he think we wouldn't care? Is that the impression we gave?

After it happened, we found out that a lot of people actually thought we'd stick by him. They thought that because we were these boisterous, obnoxious, and morally bereft lads, we wouldn't care. That we wouldn't understand why what he did was wrong.

To find out people think you don't care about rape is a sobering thing. It's not comparable to what our friend went through, obviously. But for people who know you to assume that you don't know right from wrong, or that camaraderie takes priority over something as black-and-white as sexual assault, is a kick in the balls.

It's a kick in the balls because I saw how my "toxic male" friends actually reacted. I saw the anger and the tears. I saw the shame. But most of all I saw the concern. The first priority for every single one of them was what they could do to help her. There was no debate about what should happen to him. None of them stood up for him. There were no "buts." No second chances.

When a friend dies, at least they're fucking dead. They're in the ground and the memories you have of them are untarnished and blissful. You can reminisce purely with the rose-tinted glasses of death. The ones that block out the arguments, the flaws, and the mundane.

This monster is still alive. He's out there. Due to a lack of evidence—and our friend not wishing to go through any more than she already has—he's still free. He's suffered plenty of consequences, but not enough.

This is a man who recommended my favorite book to me. We went on holiday together. He bought me dinner. He made me cry with laughter on many occasions. And I now hate him.

I don't know if the anger we all feel will ever truly go away. Every time I hang out with my woman friend, I am reminded of my own failure. She's doing absolutely fine, by the way. I feel like at this point it's best you know that she is probably the strongest person I've ever met in my life. I have done a show, called *X,* that features this whole, horrible debacle, and she helped me write it because she's incredibly funny, talented, and selfless. She makes some of the most horrific jokes about the whole thing. Jokes that are like gut punches—my favorite type. She's the best.

In hindsight, though, the signs were there. He was a dark person, which is what initially made us be friends with him. He enjoyed insults and gallows humor and drinking, so he fit in perfectly. But as time went on he was much more closed off than the rest of us. When we were all able to open up about our insecurities and fears, those rare moments when we dropped the "lads" act and had genuine heart-to-heart discussions, he never did it. Never. He always got uncomfortable and would try and turn the conversation back to banter. It was like he was actively trying to stop the rare moments of self-improvement we attempted to have.

There were also times when we saw him being creepy with girls. Nothing forceful. Just pushy. Not in an aggressive way, at least that we saw, just in a persistent way. And consistently so, in a way that when we look back on it now, we feel like utter fucking idiots for not realizing what he was.

I've also been persistent with girls. I've also sometimes accidentally been overly familiar. I've read a situation wrong and missed the mark entirely. I'm sure most men have. These memories are the ones that come back to you in the shower and somehow manage to make you shiver, despite the fact that the water is scalding hot. But it's never hot enough to burn the embarrassment and shame away.

Those similarities between the two of us terrify the fuck out of me, but the thing that keeps me sane is that I know that I know "no means no" (fucking hell, try saying that sentence out loud). I now believe my ex-friend is a legitimate psychopath. No empathy. No remorse. Out only for himself. An incredible manipulator. The way he hid it from us and managed to convince us that he wasn't what he seemed for so many years—I didn't even know that was possible.

I do know that we absolutely could have done better. Do not think this is my way of putting all of the blame on him. Some of the responsibility does fall to us. But not a lot. He was the one who decided to do what he did. It's not her fault. It's not my fault. It's not Kai's fault. It's *his* fault. He is the one that made that decision, and we are making sure that decision affects the rest of his fucking life, I assure you.

The rest of us are still reeling from it. As horrific as it is, it forced us all to take a really long look at ourselves and our behavior. Even though I still think making jokes and drinking all the time is incredibly cool and I actively encourage it, we're more aware of what we're like and what we might be encouraging, whether intentional or not. Even though we know things are just jokes and banter, others might not, and the responsibility there does fall to us.

Men need to keep other men in line because when women try to do it they're called insane. Or many worse things. I may not believe in fighting fire with fire, but I do think you should fight men with men. I, despite certain parts of the Internet, do believe that most men are good. That comes from the fact that most of the men I know are good. They are flawed, they make mistakes, and they get a lot of things wrong. But that also applies to every single person that ever existed. Except for Keanu Reeves, who is perfect in every way, and we must protect him at all costs.

If men want to be emotional, then let them be emotional. If they want to be stoic and protective, then let them be that, too. A lot of these things might be outdated, but you don't get to decide how they make blokes feel. Look at marriage proposals, for a start. Traditionally, men propose. Now we're going through a time when we're, rightfully, looking at some traditions and seeing them as outdated and pointless. That being said, I'd be gutted if my girlfriend proposed to me. Not because I don't love her, but because that's my fucking job. And not because women are property or because of the patriarchy or any of that other bullshit you're going to dump on me, but because ever since I was a little boy and I knew I wanted to get married I knew I wanted to be the one to propose.

It's in all the movies and the TV shows. My dad would tell me the story of how he proposed to my mum. Every time someone got engaged, you heard exactly how it happened and it was beautiful and romantic. Yeah, it's a fantasy of mine. It's my wedding dress.

I'm not saying women shouldn't be allowed to propose. Of course they should. If they want to. But it's one of those things that I think most men want to do. I like being seen as a protector. A lot of women could probably kick my head in if we ended up in a fight, but I still like being the big spoon. Especially when you wrap your arms and legs around your partner and fart. I call it "the jetpack."

Maybe that's one of my blind spots. One of those things that when I become an old person and my grandkids hear me say, "I proposed to your grandmother," they'll be like, "Pops! How archaic! How patriarchal! What a beast you are!"—my generation's version of casual racism.

I wouldn't be the man I am today if it weren't for my male friendships. The good and the bad ones. Some of my male friends started out as people I genuinely looked up to, and the only reason I stopped is because they improved me so much that I finally became something close to their level. A lot of the most valuable lessons I've learned came from my "boiz boiz boiz." I was made by women but I was shaped by men.

Fuck! That felt like a real definitive end there. Proper chapter-ending stuff. A quote that blokes have as their Facebook profile picture on International Women's Day, "I was made by women but shaped by men," and all the men in the comments being like, "Whoa #deep." But then I read it back and realized it's utter bollocks. I was made by only one woman, and she had a man's help in that.

Just pretend I ended on something profound.

Chapter 8

Toxic Partners and Why They Suck

Sometimes you leave a relationship on good terms. You're both able to realize that, despite the fact that you grew apart, without each other you wouldn't have grown to become the person who was emotionally intelligent enough to realize that it was time to move on. A bittersweet moment of giving up something that gave you so much, in search of something more fulfilling.

On the other hand, I hope my ex dies in a car crash. As long as no *innocent* civilians are killed, I don't think I'd bat an eye.

It was the worst relationship I've ever had in my life. You never forget your first and you never forget your worst. In hindsight, I genuinely can't think of a single good memory from it. I know there were some. There must have been. You don't get into a relationship with someone you already hate in the same way that you don't get into an ambulance that's on fire, no matter how much the paramedic convinces you that she's fully qualified and everything will be fine.

That was my ex: an on-fire ambulance. Telling me to get farther into the ambulance because that's where all the medicines are to help my burns. If only I'd just get farther into the back, then everything will be fine. The only reason I was getting burned was because I had set the fire in the first place. It was all my fault.

I understand this is extremely unfair of me to write about this relationship and not give her the chance to defend herself. I assure you that if I did give her the opportunity, she would lie through her teeth and you would believe every single word of it. I probably would, too. That's how good she is. Not since *Blade Runner* has something done such an incredible job of pretending to be a human being. Sometimes I think that perhaps it wasn't as bad as I remember. But it was. So I'm going to try and leave out as many of the bad, evil, toxic stories as I can and just explain how she made me feel. This way, at least, I can't be accused of lying about her/us/it.

There are many forms of abusive relationships, and the one I was in was on the lower end of the spectrum. It sucked, but it could have been way worse. I don't want you to think this is a "Woe is me" chapter where I compare my stubbed toe to your amputated leg. I'm just complaining about that one time I stubbed my toe on a massive cunt.

Although I'm reasonably sure it mentally scarred me for

life, it did also inspire me to write my show *Jigsaw,* which then got picked up for Netflix, which led me to get this book deal. Maybe I owe her a thank-you.* One might even be tempted to dedicate the book to her. But not me.

It wasn't physical violence. She was too smart for that; physical bruises are too easy to see. But she did manage to suck every single shred of happiness out of the core of who I am, my very being, and reduce me to a dildo that had an accent and the same opinions she did. For someone who loves himself so greatly, I have to commend this woman for making me hate myself more than any Ecstasy comedown I've ever had.

Emotional abuse is tough because it takes you ages to realize what's going on. Physical violence is horrific, but at least you know when you've been punched. There is blood. There are bruises. There is an impact. Your brain goes, "Fucking ow!," and lets you know that something has gone terribly wrong and that you are in danger.

Emotional abuse can take ages to settle in. Sometimes you're not even sure it's happened. Imagine if your body didn't bruise and someone kept hitting you. Now imagine how easy it would be for your partner to convince you that he or she hadn't hit you at all. That you were imagining things. Proving emotional abuse is so hard, you can't actually see it, and that's why it's so dangerous.

* She owes me months of my life and thousands of pounds in therapy, so we'll call it even.

My friends and family had no idea how miserable I was. She kept up such a wonderful appearance in public. Beautiful, friendly, selfless, thoughtful, great tits. All the personality traits she had learned to mimic and emulate in order to get what she wanted. Then, the second no one else was watching, it was time for her to remove the mask and drop the act. My friends and family would tell me how perfect she was. How well I'd done for myself. I was punching above my weight.

If you blindfold someone and hold a slice of apple under his nose, not only are you an absolute fucking weirdo, but if you then put a slice of onion in that person's mouth, his brain will convince him it's an apple. One trustworthy sense is telling him it's an apple, so it must be an apple. When enough evidence points to something, no matter how ludicrous it is, you begin to believe it. So if enough people who you love tell you someone is great, you believe them. Despite all the evidence to the contrary. It makes you feel broken for not seeing what they see. When, in actual fact, the problem is that they can't see what you see.

Now, in her defense, I don't think she has any idea how much of an absolute cunt she was. Cunts don't know they're cunts. If they did, they wouldn't be cunts. They think other people are cunts. Cunts are weird like that. I don't necessarily think that she was vindictive or spiteful or that she did all of this intentionally. I don't think she planned things or compared notes with other monsters who took abject pleasure in reducing everyone close to them into a shell of their former selves so they were easier to mold to fit their narcissistic endeavors. I think it just came naturally to her. And I do respect raw talent.

Then again, maybe she did know what she was doing. Some of it certainly seemed tactical. Making sure that I never got enough sleep so that I wouldn't have the energy to argue with her. Making me go through my sexual history and explaining to me why I was a gross, disgusting, horrible man and why I should be ashamed of the fact that I thought it was all okay. Carefully calculating ways to make me hate the person I was before she was kind enough to step into my life and fix me. Trying to turn me against anyone who I seemed to love more than I loved her: my best friends Jean, Kai, and Ally; my parents; Chelsea Football Club.

It's tough not to still hate her. I hate what she made me. I hate what she reduced me to. I hate the doubt she filled me with. I see the shit-covered footprints of her cuntery in my new relationship. The psychological aftershocks of her cancerous attitudes. I keep apologizing for things I don't need to apologize for. My current girlfriend finds it funny. "Why on earth are you apologizing for not answering my drunken phone call at three a.m.?" It's hard to explain to her that that used to be a death sentence.

Mainly, it's also hard not to hate *myself*. I think that's where most of the resentment comes from. The self-loathing she makes me feel. It's embarrassing to fall in love with someone who is a shit. At the start of the relationship you're besotted with this person. Infatuated beyond reason.

Convinced they're "the One." Telling all your friends how perfect and brilliant this person is. Then you realize that the best meal you've ever had in your life was literally shit on a plate. You've eaten shit in front of all your friends and you just have to smile through it, brown teeth and everything. It damages your pride.

I'm ashamed of the fact that I started neglecting some of my friends because she told me to. I thought I was stronger than that. Smarter than that. Better than that. Not that pathetic type of human being who does what he's told, no matter what. That's for weak people.

The people in those situations might not be weak at all, but I assure you that they *feel* weak. That's what these types of relationships can do to the human ego. No matter the strength of a person, it's hard to defend yourself against someone who you think is on your side. Someone who takes advantage of your empathy. Your trust. Your kindness. They use those things against you and afterward you're left hating the only things that you ever loved about yourself.

I cringe at how obvious all this was, now that I look back on it through shattered rose-tinted glasses. How easy I was to manipulate, like putty in her hands. That's what manipulators do, though. They hate themselves, so they make you hate yourself. Instead of accepting your offers to try and make them love themselves, it's much easier to drag you down to their level of self-immolation. It's kamikazes love.

Then, when you finally hate yourself, they love you.

They're so kind to you. What sort of person loves a piece of shit like you? A saint, that's who. It's brilliant. They isolate you, make you hate yourself, and then tell you how much they love you, which blows your mind. This person loves you despite all of your flaws. They're willing to get past all of those negative things, the ones you weren't aware of until they graciously pointed them out, and still be with you. This angel is willing to love you, in spite of all the reasons they just told you that made you unlovable.

It also makes you not trust yourself. Every time you feel anything close to love again you try to push it away. You remember exactly what happened last time you felt like this and there isn't a chance you're going to be stupid enough to let it happen again. You get all Trumped up and build some walls.

My current relationship is in its fairly early days and it's bliss. It's that joyous period in the relationship when we love everything about each other and haven't discovered each other's gaping flaws. She has no idea how much I love Adam Sandler's *The Longest Yard*,* and I hope she never will.

The only thing ruining this wonderful, cathartic, purifying love is the fact that I don't trust it. Last time I felt like this, it took me quite literally years to recover. Obviously, to compare the two of them—current and ex—is to compare

---

* It's an absolutely brilliant sporting underdog movie with a stellar cast of comedians, professional wrestlers, and rappers. If you didn't enjoy it, that's on you for walking in expecting anything other than a fun Adam Sandler movie. You fun sponge.

a cute puppy filled with love and adoration to an assassin who kills by punching you in the dick of your soul in front of all of your friends.

It's tough to get out of those relationships, because your self-worth is at an all-time low. It's like a bank keeping you in debt. People hate being alone so much that they'll take something bad over nothing at all. They're floating on a lonely raft in the middle of the ocean and they're so dehydrated they decide to drink the seawater. It's a brief moment of respite that makes everything worse.

It's important to learn how to be alone and to be fine with it. I'm great at being alone because my job creates it. I travel around the world doing gigs, so most of my time is spent with myself. It gets lonely, but you learn to tolerate your own company. You get used to it. And then you start to like it.

Some people are so bad at being alone, so terrified of the thoughts in their own head, that they need to distract themselves with another person. I can't relate to that. I'm fortunate enough to not have depression. I don't mean that to sound horrible, but I have a lot of friends with depression and it looks fucking *brutal*. I can't imagine having a brain that constantly tells you that you suck. My brain thinks I'm excellent. It's an enabler. Even when I do something bad, my brain is there, saying, "Mistakes happen, bro. You didn't mean it. Don't beat yourself up. Love you."

My mates have brains that are cunts and I have to watch them fight this constant, ongoing war in their own heads.

One of my closest friends has depression. He is one of the kindest, most thoughtful, funniest people I know. Yet his brain keeps telling him he's worthless. If any person made my friend feel that way, I'd kick the living shit out of him. But I can't beat up the perpetrator in this instance because he's also the victim. It's a real catch-22.*

If I could get them to somehow break up with their brain, I would. I'd say, "Look, it's not working out between you two. I know you had some good times a couple of years ago, but the positive memories are few and far between."

It's hard to know if I regret the horrible relationship I had. On one hand, I absolutely fucking do. She was a despicable human being, she will do what she did to me to some other sad sack, and I'll say nothing because better him than me.

On the other side, it's the relationship that made me write *Jigsaw,* and I've seen the impact that show has had. It's easy for people to focus on the fact that the show broke up more than 120,000 couples, resulted in 350 engagements being canceled and more than 300 divorces, because that's what I keep telling everyone. When people hear the statistics or read the clickbait articles about the show, it's easy for them to dismiss it as "How dumb are these people who broke up because of this comedian?" or "He's a sociopath." I agree with both sentiments, by the way.

Having spoken to a lot of the people who did break

* I've never read *Catch-22.* I'm just trying to fit in.

up because of the show has really changed my outlook on what I went through. I've spoken to thousands of other people who were in toxic relationships. Bullying relationships. Abusive relationships. And, as crazy as it is, *Jigsaw* did help give them the courage to get out and stay out of that relationship.

It's the staying out that's the hard part. These manipulative fucks will do anything they can to stay in your life once you are no longer in the relationship, because they are terrified of you. They are terrified because you saw them without the mask. You saw who they truly are. You've witnessed their toxic, Chernobyl core of hate and you survived it. That fills them with dread because it means you can then tell everyone what an absolute bastard they were and they don't have the skill to spin that tale. Their lies do not work anymore. They'll do whatever it takes to weasel their way back into your life and I thoroughly recommend not letting them.

I've spoken to an incredible woman who works at a shelter for abused women. She showed *Jigsaw* to her group, and afterward she saw a dramatic rise in the number of women who stayed out of their abusive relationships. Never in a million years did I ever think I'd have an impact like that. I was just hoping to make my ex hate herself one iota of how much she made me hate myself.

So it's hard to regret the shitty relationship. I'm better for it. Other people are better for it. She's still alive, but you can't win them all.

As chance would have it, she has just texted me as I am writing this. I swear, her horns must have been burning. I haven't seen her in five years, but I attempted to clear the air with her awhile ago. More for me than anything else.

I couldn't stand carrying around that hatred and fear any longer. Those two things go hand in hand. We hate being scared so we hate what scares us. I was terrified of her for years and years. All the things that she could still do from the outside to fuck my life up. To continue to hurt me.

Jean saw it in me. Every time I spoke about my ex I did it with such passionate venom that she could tell I wished my words were literal daggers. Jean knew it wasn't good for my mental health, because she knows how much hate I am capable of.

I've never understood these hippies who say things like, "Hate takes up so much space in your brain, it's not worth it." Shut it, Gandhi. The brain's capacity is infinite. Thoughts and feelings are immeasurable. You can't fill something infinite. If you fart in space, all of space doesn't smell like farts. Read a science book.

Apparently, though, some people do have limited brain space. When they hate someone it takes up 50 percent of their brain, so for half of the day they're focused on hating that one person and they can't focus on meditating or drinking sparkling water out of a fucking jam jar while reading Tarot cards and star signs. That's when they get all holier-than-thou, "I find hate is just such a waste of time."

Do you, cunt? That's interesting, because it fucking fuels me and you just became petroleum.

You think you're better than me because you don't hate people? Strap in, shitehawk, I'm gonna hate you for the rest of my life and it won't even take up a second of my day. It's called multitasking, you linear-brained moron. Can you also not pat your head and rub your tummy at the same time?

Hating someone all the time doesn't take up brain space. I didn't sit there for years hating her every single day, unable to function with the sheer force of contempt rushing around my brain. I would be doing something, someone would mention her name, and I'd go, "Oh, yeah, I wish she was dead." And then I'd just go back to baking cakes or having my wank. Hating her comes as naturally as breathing to me.

That being said, it was exhausting. Not the hate. The fear. I was so scared of her for so long. I built her up to be a thousand times worse than she probably ever truly was, and I think Jean saw that. Jean definitely also hated her and knew she was a pile of shit. But I think Jean saw a human pile of shit, rather than the soul-sucking succubus that I saw. Jean always sees the best in people.

She convinced me that I didn't have to be best friends with this person ever again, but that I was carrying around a lot of issues from the relationship and it was going to hamper me in the rest of my life unless I did something to sort it out. So I got drunk with Jean and we sent the Evil One a message explaining why I felt the way I felt. Saying that it was all water under the bridge. My ex was obviously apologetic, sincere, understanding, and all those other fucking lies that she's so good at. It's hard to know whether she is telling the truth. Whether she earnestly feels these things or whether she's just learned what to say in order to save face. I will never know.

So why did she just text me right now? I think she just wants that meet-up. She knows how much I have vilified her in my own head (rightfully), and she wants to humanize herself to me. Quite frankly, I can't be bothered. I don't owe her anything and I don't want to spend any amount of time with the only person who ever made me want to kill myself. I think I'm well within my rights to feel that way.

Perhaps she'll read this one day and recognize just how toxic it was, but that would probably require a level of self-awareness that she didn't show for a second during the time we were together. Part of me wants that. In some sick, twisted, vengeful way, I want her to hate herself as much as she made me hate myself. There's no point, though. She probably already does. People who do horrible things are very rarely in a good space when they do them. I'm sure she has some valid excuses for her behavior. She also has multiple made-up excuses that she throws out whenever there is a chance to spin herself as a victim. Maybe she even interpreted the situation in a different way. Sociopaths often do.

The nicest thing I can say about her is that I hope she gets the help she needs. I hope she gets better. Not for her. Not for me. But for the poor, innocent man whose heart she burrows into next.

I blame Hollywood for most of this. Every single thing ever created for movies and TV has love interests for every character along the way. Everyone eventually finds love. Even Phoebe Buffay, the most unlovable character ever created.*

The reason they do this is because love is the most important thing in the world. With it you feel amazing, and without it you turn into all the people you hate. I guarantee you that all the politicians you loathe were never truly loved by their parents or family. The absence of love creates those we find unlovable.

It makes sense to put happy endings in so many movies. Making sure that we realize that everyone deserves love and that it's important and blah blah blah. Unfortunately, TV shows and movies are famously shorter than real life. They cram a lot of shit into that brief period of time and get rid of all the scenes where nothing really happens. This gives us all a false sense of urgency. "Oh, my God, Katherine Heigl absolutely hated Gerard Butler at the start of this movie. He was an obnoxious jackass, but now look. In just over

---

* There is nothing endearing, lovable, or enjoyable about willful ignorance.

ninety minutes they have changed and grown to love each other. I must do the same."

We rush into these things because we're terrified of being alone. Hollywood has never really made being alone look good. It's always a tough, brooding man who hasn't known the touch of a woman since he lost his wife to ISIS/cancer/random murder. Now he's waging a one-man war. Or it's a strict businesswoman who is just too busy to be in a relationship and look how she holds a baby—oh, my God, she'll never be a wife or a mother.

They never show you the scenes of that brooding man sitting in peace, not having to listen to a story about three women from his wife's work who he has allegedly met and what sort of inane office drama they are all involved in. Hollywood has never shown a scene of that businesswoman satisfying herself with the eleventh setting on her vibrator in the middle of the living room, knowing full well some snot-nosed little brat isn't going to come in asking for a PB&J and a bedtime story.

Loneliness is like most things in the world: You have to practice it to get good at it. Sometimes being alone is utter bliss. Once you get used to being alone, relationships really have to go out of their way to interest you. If you want to be in a relationship with me, you have to be better than being single.

So many toxic relationships exist and are allowed to thrive because none of us are much good at being lonely. Having something awful is better than having nothing at all. I'm not criticizing the logic. I get it. A rotten apple core while you're starving is better than nothing. But don't eat shit food for the rest of your life.

Being alone teaches you a lot about yourself. Like how many times you can masturbate before your dick makes more noise when you cum than you do. It isn't always the best thing in the world, but it's better than the company of most people who live in Florida. There have been so many times in life when I've been in a conversation with someone and thought, *I'd rather be alone than go through this.*

I think the problem with loneliness is that lonely people tend to consume things to make them feel even more alone. They'll listen to music about heartbreak, turn on rom-coms in order to taunt themselves with what they could have, or watch porn. The more people in the porn you're watching, the lonelier you are—I think it was Nelson Mandela who said that.

If you're lonely and not enjoying it, I suggest that you walk into any city center and just people-watch. Really look at and study passersby, especially ones in relationships, and pay attention to how miserable some of them are. Better yet, go onto Facebook and look into the lives of every person you went to school with who settled down at twenty-one. On the surface, their posts and pictures are happy. Of course they are. They're edited. They're designed to make you think that they're living a wonderful life so that you don't get to see the insurmountable sadness that consumes these people as they spend every waking moment of their adult life with the human being their teenage self chose.

I don't know about you, but I was a fucking moron when I was a teenager. I'd hate to be held accountable or to be obligated to any decision my teenage self made. Would you let your teenage self pick your car? Fuck no. Would you give your teenage self your credit card? Not a fucking chance. I can barely trust thirty-year-old me with a credit card. So can you imagine how awful it is to spend your entire life with the first moron that was ever dumb enough to shag you? You don't have to imagine, I'll tell you. It must be miserable.

If you wish to know how much I hit the nail on the head there, show that passage to anyone who got married under twenty-one and look how angry and defensive they get. Trust me.

All insults aside, the only reason I go so hard at this is because I remember the purity of the sheer joy I felt once I got out of my toxic relationship. It was one of the greatest moments of my life. Utter, liberating freedom from someone who, according to other people, "isn't that bad." I want others to feel that. To share that relief. If you are truly happy in your relationship with your high school sweetheart, congratulations and this chapter isn't about you. I swear.

If you're thinking of getting out of a toxic relationship, there is one bit of information I would like to remind you about—the other person is not your responsibility. At all. In any way, shape, or form. No matter what he or she will tell you. If they threaten to kill themselves, let them. Do nothing. Let them cry, scream, yell, and beg, and if they want to do themselves in, let them. Good riddance.

I have friends who are too scared to break up with their emotionally manipulative partners because they're so terrified about the ramifications of the breakup. "If I leave him, I don't know how he'll handle it." Good news. You don't have to be there to see it. That's entirely his fucking problem. You're not a couple anymore.

Other people have to be able to handle their own shit, and if they can't—well, that sucks for them. Not your problem. You owe nothing to anyone other than yourself. You should still strive to be kind, strive to be good, try your hardest to be the best human being you possibly can. But if someone takes advantage of your empathy by using it against you and holding you hostage by telling you that without you they'll kill themselves, then press the "top floor" button for them in the elevator, shove them in, grab an umbrella, and leave.

The type of people who do this do need help. I understand that. I hope they find it. It is not your responsibility, though. You are not their therapist, and if you are, then you should lose your license. Come on, now. Don't shit where you eat.

Suggest places for them to get help, let their family or

friends know, but make sure you wash your hands of them. Send them on the right path, and if they fall off of it— fuck 'em. Otherwise two people lose their lives, sitting in a relationship based on nothing but fear, guilt, self-loathing, and hate.

Another important note: Most people who threaten to kill themselves don't. People who are actually depressed and genuinely suicidal tend to be very quiet about it. That's why it's so hard to prevent and why it's devastating to hear. When most people commit suicide, you think, *Oh, my God. I had no idea.* Robin Williams, Anthony Bourdain, Chris Cornell. All their suicides came as a shock because they didn't threaten it every single chance they got.

These people who threaten it as a form of revenge are attention-seeking. They want a reaction and they'll do anything they can to get one. But, much like toddlers, the second you stop paying attention to them there's little else they can do.

Suicide is a brutal thing. Though I think it should be made easier. If you want to die, I think you're well within your right to do so. As long as you're of sound mind when you make the choice, if it's illness-related or pain-related or anything like that—then who am I to tell you no? Who is anyone to tell you how easy your suffering might be? I think you should go to therapy for a couple months, and if at the end of that you still want to commit suicide, then we'll find a fun way to do it. Fire you out of a cannon.

Feed you to a shark. Tie your legs and arms to two different horses and pull you like a Christmas cracker. It's genuinely your choice. Go out with a bang.

If you are suicidal and reading this, please do talk to someone. I promise you that you are more loved than you think. Even I love you. Sure, it might just be because you bought this book and are a fan of mine. But it's still love, and beggars can't be choosers.*

Threatening suicide to get your own way is emotional blackmail at its darkest level and it does not get discussed enough, because these emotionally manipulative narcissists are so very clever and subtle at what they do. It eats away at the soul of the other person. What a burden to hold over someone else. To make them genuinely believe that their actions will result in your death. Monstrous.

Anyway, I hope you enjoyed this chapter, and if you complain about it, I'll fucking kill myself.

* I'm kidding. You are loved, you fucking idiot.

Chapter 9

The Pandemic: I Fought
My Thoughts and My Thoughts Won

It's hard to be humble when you're brilliant. You'll have to take my word for it. The pressure is enormous, but that's my cross to bear. Whenever I see people claim to be humble I always think, *Of course you are. I'd be humble, too, if I were you.* You have nothing to be arrogant about. It's like saying, "I didn't even want to go!" to a party you weren't invited to. It's easy to be celibate when no one wants to fuck you. So I've heard.

I'm not confident about everything—that would be delusional. I have no misguided thoughts on my prowess as an athlete. I once knocked myself out before a high school game of soccer (I hate calling it that—may God have mercy on my soul) because I ran into the goalposts during warm-up. My team of brave underdogs beat two other teams to win the house cup. (I'm aware that to American readers it probably sounds like I went to Hogwarts. I wish. Ravenclaw for life, baby.) I wasn't there to lift the trophy myself as I was being treated for what the doctors called "a minor head wound at most, you big wimp. I honestly can't believe you insisted on being stretchered here."

I'm also very humble about my abilities as a chef. I can cook a few good meals that would impress a first or second date. So why learn a third? If we haven't had sex by that point, you belong to a religion that I don't have the time to pretend to respect. Compared to someone who has a passion and love for cooking, I'm the equivalent of a paint-by-numbers artist. No creativity—just good at staying inside the lines. Speaking of, I'm also shit at painting and drawing. I'm not artistically talented. Or musically. According to my mother, I couldn't carry a tune in a bucket. I once got fired from Pantomime for being such a horrible singer.

For those of you who don't know, a Pantomime, or Panto, is a traditional Christmas production that takes place in every single theater across the UK during the winter holiday season. Each production is based on a different well-known kids' tale—"Snow White and the Seven Dwarfs," "Cinderella," etc. It's a two-to-three-hour-long extravaganza of terrible songs, cheap jokes for the adults, and lots of minor celebrities being booked in for six-week runs as they try to remain relevant by playing the genie in Stoke-on-Trent's production of *Aladdin*. Yours truly was booked to play the comic relief in Aladdin alongside David Hasselhoff, Pamela Anderson, and Brian Blessed. No, I'm not kidding. And *I* was the one who was asked to leave after three days because my singing was so horrendous I would have made those titans of the theater look bad.

I'm going to be VERY humble about this book because I haven't written one before. I enjoyed writing it. A lot. It's been a fucking joy. That doesn't mean people will enjoy reading it. In the same way that just because you might enjoy wanking on someone doesn't necessarily mean they enjoy being wanked on (God, I'm such a feminist). Everyone who has read it, so far, has enjoyed it. But they were family, friends, and publishers, and they all have to say that because they know that as a white man I run strictly on ego. I don't have innate confidence in my ability as a writer. It's new to me. If this book gets panned, I'll obviously be hurt, but only about the book. It won't bleed into the other parts of my life. I'll have a little cry, write down the names of all the critics who panned it, find out who they are, where they live, where they work, and any other tidbits I can scour from the Internet, and then I'll wait. Five, ten, twenty years. Who knows? I'll wait. Patiently. Long enough for them to forget. I'll sit down and commit the list to memory nightly, like Arya Stark.

One day they'll be dropping off their grandchild at the school gates. Waving goodbye. One last time. Not that they'll know that. As they trudge through the snow on the lonely, widow-walk back to their dingy cabin, they'll stop at something. Some sort of message. Pissed into the snow. They'll take out their reading glasses, hands shaking from both the cold and their Parkinson's. Dry lips mumbling the words "'Charmless, aggressive, and devoid of laughter?' . . . Why, that's what I said about . . . My God!" Too late. Their hearing aid picks it up just a second too late. A familiar sound. But all this dementia up in their brain isn't allowing them to register what the noise is. The shaking gets worse. Wait. That's not *them* shaking . . . That's the ground. Oh, my God. They look up and see it. Their doom. The Monster Truck, which I paid for with the advance on this book, rumbling toward them. The corpse of their deceased partner dug up, taxidermized, and adorning the grill like a fucked-up mermaid on the bow of a ship, smashing through their brittle, brittle bones. United one last time. At sixty miles per hour. A perfect story arc. Then I'll gleefully hand out free copies of this book, which I got from the bargain bins in charity shops, to any onlookers.

Or I'll just get back to what I know I'm good at—comedy.

Which I am VERY good at. One of the best. There is genuinely nothing you could do to convince me otherwise. People have tried. It happens on the Internet all the time. Plebs stumble across my stand-up and choose to take it personally. As if I've ever even given the faintest of shits about the thoughts of anyone lonely enough to Google my name. The weakest insult of all time to hurl at a comedian is the phrase "so-called comedian." Motherfucker, I live in a house paid for by dick jokes. Pipe the fuck down. I'm so good at my "so-called" job that I own "so-called" property, have a "so-called" supercar, get to travel the "so-called" world, and have had "so-called" sex with several "so-called" women . . . wait, this has gone terribly wrong.

My simple point is, I'm better than you in every fucking way.

Or at least that's what I think the opening to this chapter would have been had 2020 not gone the way it did. Had my giant, insufferable ego not been so thoroughly popped last year, what you just read could easily have been sincere. Hell, some of it still is (the Monster Truck bit). After I wrote that opening, I immediately read it out to my girlfriend with no context because I love to test the boundaries of love and acceptance. I got to watch her love for me slowly leave her body, through her eyes, in a way that made me sympathize with Chris Pratt, as I imagine it's how every woman he has ever opened up to has reacted. "You . . . You believe what? But I loved *Parks and Rec.* How could you be so stupid? This is horrible. You're so handsome—PLEASE STOP PRAYING, CHRIS. YOU'RE JUST MAKING IT WORSE!"

It turns out that if you spend most of your late teens and all of your twenties focusing on your dream career, then you, unwittingly, get all of your self-worth from your job. Which is fine. Great, in fact, for the most part. Walking onstage to a room full of strangers who cheer with utter delight at your mere presence is an EXCELLENT way to live. Until there is a global pandemic that causes the entire world to shut down and suddenly there isn't a room full of strangers to validate your existence anymore. It's just *you* doing that, and you haven't done that for years, mate.

Without an audience, there is no Netflix– and HBO– Daniel Sloss. There's only Daniel. Danny to his mates. DJ to his parents. Shagmaster General to his beloved. Sloss-balls M.D. to several homeless men in the area, though not as many as there used to be. I haven't spent much time with DJ since he was an unsure, scared sixteen-year-old who thought he might give stand-up comedy a shot. That little dweeb. God, he was such a nervous wreck. Anxious about everything but not understanding that it was anxiety. Trying so hard to be loved by everyone. Telling himself, *Don't worry, little buddy. One day they'll love you.* And that confidence will go straight to your head. It'll become a drug. Then drugs will become drugs. You'll enjoy those, too.

I've never had to question my mental health. It's always been great. Very solid. My inner monologue was my best friend for most of my life. A proper internal hype man. I'd come off stage and my brain would say, "Excellent job there, Daniel. Another killer gig. You are truly fucking good at this." Thanks, Brain. Love you, too.

I'd see a girl after a show, and my brain would say, "I've run through all the scenarios, and there does not exist a world where she is not gagging for a shagging." Thanks, Brain, I'm on it. What a wingman.

The girl would walk away, fake smile on her face, and my brain would be like, "Nailed. It. We're not even going to read into the fact that the number she gave you is three digits short, and she claimed her name was 'Fire exit'—you absolutely smashed that, lad." Thanks, Brain you're the best!

Even when I fucked up, my brain would still be on my side. I'd forget a friend's birthday or name, upset an audience member with a crude joke or something that hit way too close to home, waste an entire day smoking weed and playing computer games, and STILL my brain would be like, "Fucking hell, Sloss. You do life so fucking well, mate. FUCK YES." THANK YOU, BRAIN! I KNOW!

Even in moments where I wasn't confident, wasn't sure of myself, and had some of those pesky doubts, I had fans. Even in the moments where my massive ego couldn't do the heavy lifting on all my deep-rooted flaws, the fans showed up. Fans that told me everything I needed to hear, "You're great . . . You're brilliant . . . I love you . . . Sir, I just work here, please stop signing my mop." They just kept heaping fuel and coal onto the fire of the uncut arrogance burning deep inside my chest.

I came back to Edinburgh after doing shows in L.A. in March 2020. Shows that went really well, I might add. Within two days of returning to Scotland, we were at the start of a fifteen-week lockdown. I quickly found out another thing I am quite bad at—the traditional Scottish pastime of doing fuck all. I'm very bad at doing nothing. I don't mean that I'm like those lunatics who wake up at 4:30 a.m., eat ten eggs, run a marathon, build a house from scratch, and then write a fourteen-page Instagram tirade about how "Procrastination is my enemy! Always be working! Never slow down! Susan, please come back. It's all for nothing without you and the kids. Please, just call. Please. Susan, please. WORK HARD. PLAY HARDER. Make life your bitch." Bless those people, and I hope whatever demons loudly plague their minds quiet down one day. Mainly so I don't have to feel bad about how little I do.

I'm actually very good at doing nothing, I'm just not good at not reprimanding myself for doing nothing. I was excited by the concept of "time off." Especially at the end of an eighteen-month tour. Normally, I'll have four weeks off where I just cram in as much "doing nothing" as I can because I know I'll be back on the road again soon. Weed, beanbag, games console, Netflix, junk food, recharge, bliss. Oh, and cuddling with my girlfriend, if she's reading this. But thanks to COVID, this was going to be *extended* time off. No end in sight. Surely, I'd nail it.

Wrong. That same inner monologue that had been telling me that I was God's gift to the world suddenly processed my time off as unemployment and changed its tune to a much sadder one. One that belonged on an Adele album. "You could be writing a sitcom . . .* You're not read-

* The bane of my fucking life is being asked to write a sitcom. I do not want to write a sit-com. I am a comedian. I do stand-up comedy. If you want a sitcom, then I highly suggest you find a writer. I can do comedy, and I'll try acting if you write a character with a Scottish accent. Otherwise, go find someone that enjoys sitting down for extended periods of time, writing and rewriting and rewriting in order to try and put part of their soul onto a bit of paper, which is then at the mercy of a bunch of execs who have never told a joke successfully in their entire life nor even deigned to create something instead of desperately trying to sell something that they have only a rudimentary understanding of because all they get from art is

ing enough . . . You're not working out enough . . . You speak only one language. Learn French . . . You're not doing enough . . . *You* are not enough!"

Why would I not trust that voice? That voice had been right my entire life! I'd listened to every single insidious thought I'd had and believed every word. So in 2020 I sat making myself feel guilty about my own existence, thinking that in order to be happy I had to utilize all this time off, to be as efficient with it as possible.

Don't get me wrong, most of my job is actually doing absolutely fucking hee-haw (Scottish for nada), but it's well disguised as doing a lot. I have the aura of someone who works hard. The fact that I have to travel much of the time gives people the illusion that I'm a hard worker as opposed to a perpetually hungover man who gets picked up by a car, dropped off at an airport, led onto an airplane, picked up from a different airport, driven to a venue, handed a glass of whisky, and then goes onto a stage to say pretty much the exact same thing he said twenty-three hours ago. RAW. FUCKING. TALENT. BABY.

My actual job consists of working only up to ninety minutes a night. There's just a lot of travel to get to the next place to do it again. If people want to call that hard work,

---

the price tag it fetches and not the emotion it inspires nor the impact it can have. I cannot express to you how frustrating it is for some cunt from the BBC to watch an entire room full of people laugh at what you do and the only thought to cross his mind is *How do I get that person to make me something that makes me money, since I have zero talent of my own to do it.* When a person signs a contract for the BBC, you can literally see every free thought being sucked out of his head through his ass. LET. IT. ROT.

thank you. It isn't. But sincerely, thank you. Waking up after five hours of a marijuana-aided booze slumber to have to go through Paris Charles de Gaulle—an airport where the job interview process is holding an infant underwater in front of its distraught mother in order to prove that you have the correct level of empathy to work there—and then to have to stand behind old foreign couples who haven't been in an airport since 9/11 and so are bewildered as to the point of a long, slow, mundane conversation about the newfangled rules of not being allowed belts and hacksaws on an aircraft, all while I frantically lick my phone screen clean in order both to avoid jail time and get that little extra pick me up in order to sprint to the gate to make the first of four flights that day isn't exactly an easy twenty-four hours, but let's not pretend I don't spend 80 percent of it sleeping or on my phone. Just like a pilot.

I fall for the illusion, too. When I'm on the road, that voice pats me on the back, going, "God, you're such a hard worker. All this traveling the world—being driven places and drinking every night is EXHAUSTING! Such a martyr for the craft. Have your fifth wank of the day, you've earned it."

Suddenly, here I am, home for the foreseeable future, and those fifteen hours I normally spend being a lazy piece of shit are no longer disguised as a lot of work because I'm not constantly moving. Spending three hours on your phone in an airport makes you feel less bored. Spending three hours on your phone on a beanbag when there are things to be done makes you feel like a useless cunt. There's nothing else to do in an airport. There's loads I should be doing at home. Like writing this book. I've had six months to finish writing this, and I've still left it to the last minute. Pressure helps everyone do things better. If you don't believe that, go time yourself on a run. Then I'll time you as a man chases you with a machete. I wonder under which condition you'll perform better. Fun fact—that's both how Oscar Pistorius was trained and how he lost his legs.

For months I found myself getting into a downward spiral where there was nothing to do, so I'd laze around, smoke some weed, and scroll the Internet. And I'm not sure if you've been on the Internet, but it's a place where literally everyone else is doing more than you yet somehow, simultaneously, everything is going wrong constantly at all times.

I started to berate myself for having the audacity to be sad when I knew other people were having it worse. Which is an absolutely batshit mental way to try to process emotions. It's very common, though. I bet you do it, too, you fucking idiot. "Well, I'm having a hard time at the moment, but it's not as bad as so-and-so who is going through all this PLUS these extra things." Ah yes, turning emotions into a competition. How incredibly healthy. I can't see how this could ever go wrong.

Imagine your best friend turns up pounding on your front door; you barely have a moment to take in her red, tear-stained eyes as she throws her arms around your neck and weeps heavily into your chest. In between the sobs and the "there there"s, she manages to tell you that her mother just died in a car accident. Heartbreaking. Awful. Tragic. I very much doubt your reaction would be to open up the obituary of the local newspaper and say, "It could be a lot worse. See how many babies died yesterday? Three. You think your mum is better than three babies? When it comes to loss, you've experienced nothing."

There are people who live like that. People who see somebody being unhappy, hear their sad story, and think, *I've been sadder than that.* As if grief negates grief as opposed to compounding it. Instead of bonding over being sad, they want to argue semantics. Be sad about whatever you want to be sad about, and don't let anyone tell you otherwise. I was infinitely more heartbroken by the death of Ryan Dunn than I was about Princess Diana. I can't imagine what Ryan must have done to piss the Queen off that much.

In the first few months of lockdown, I didn't even realize I was in a spiral. It wasn't until I looked back, reflected upon it, and understood, "I don't think those days spent drinking whisky in a beanbag watching YouTube videos of dogs being reunited with their owners was a happy place." Had some good fucking cries, though.

Only Future You knows if you are currently nailing life or whether you're having a shitter. I signed myself up to therapy in January 2020, as if I were psychic. I don't know if some deep part of me has a spiritual connection to me from the future and he was just sending messages back in time to my subconscious saying, "You're not gonna wanna do this alone, bud. Time to emotionally lube up." But it just felt right.

I felt like I'd lost a big part of myself on tour. Mainly the part of me that liked other people. The part of me that tolerated my mates and didn't want to take a baseball bat to the skull of any friend who had the gall to text me asking for a moment of my time when I was quite clearly using all of that time wallowing in my own self-pity. So I Googled "therapy in Edinburgh" and sent an email that essentially said, "I'm a big sad boy now, waa waa wee waa." Then several crying face emojis followed by the sunglasses emoji so they knew to sign me up to a celebrity therapist and not one of the bottom-shelf corduroy shoulders to cry on that you normies have.*

I think when a lot of people hear the word *therapy,* their imagination goes a little bit wild. They envision lying on a couch while some European wearing glasses down at the farthest end of his nose says, "And how does that make you feel?" while showing you a bunch of blobs that look a hell of a lot like someone hitting Mitch McConnell with a 2x4. No, wait. 4x4. 2x4? Which one is the truck? That one. Let him get hit by a truck. You know what? Why not both? The blobs look like Mitch McConnell being hit by a 4x4. Into a tree, but it doesn't kill him, just severs him in half. Like in the movie *Signs.* But instead of Mel Gibson coming along and being all like, "I don't know if I'm ready to be a dad without you. Also, while I'm here, fuck the Jews," it's just a long line of American people trying to joust holes

---

* None of that is true, I just signed up for a regular therapist. But it's been a while since I've had the "Daniel Sloss" boots on. Lemme have my fun.

into Mitch's neckless neck with the bluntest end of a bit of wood.*

I had some reservations about therapy, but only the stupid ones that we've already discussed. I was worried my problem wasn't as big as other people's problems. Part of me thought I'd be sat in a therapist's chair, telling him about how miserable I'd been on some of the tour or how I was worried that I'd broken myself to all human emotions, while he coughed the word *pussy* under his breath and at the end was like, "Oh I'm sorry. Were your diamond shoes too tight? Hold on while I get the shoe-making elves in to fix that right up. Snap, Crackle, Pop, GET IN HERE! Sharon, can you clear all my PTSD and Sexual Assault Survivors today? Yeah, no, I'm too busy here with Macaulay Culkin and Ellen's child-star son who found it really difficult enjoying all his dreams come true. What's that? Great idea. No. I have it here. It's in the tiniest violin case, where else would it be?"

Therapy is just like putting a condom on the dick of life before it fucks you up the ass in a way that is devoid not only of love but(t) also of tenderness and spit. Therapy isn't going to stop life's being brutal and hard. But it will make it less likely that life gives you a condition that causes you to rot silently from the inside out. It's about being able to be honest about yourself while trying your absolute hardest to make your therapist laugh. They'll tell you that's not

* I'm not saying I want that to happen! I'm just saying that's what the blobs look like! Jeez!

what the actual purpose is. That what you're doing is wasting their time—and therefore yours—with a self-defense mechanism, out of fear that other people will see your flaws and because you're so desperate for approval that you're willing to have anything in common with someone, even if that thing is hating yourself.

Nevertheless, I have made him laugh several times. Sloss one, therapy nil.

The truth is my therapist hasn't dismantled my sense of humor or made me go back to all my traumatic moments to try to understand where all my worries come from. He just listens in an unbiased way, asks questions that make me self-reflect, AND he laughs at my jokes. I cannot stress this enough. He finds me very funny. Very. I swear.

Imagine your brain is like a house. With lots of different rooms and halls and corridors and attics. Pictures of fond memories line the walls; some parts are messy, but in general it's a nice place. Unfortunately, there's a small fire alarm going off. Probably just a low battery, right? You can ignore it. It goes off only occasionally, and at this point you're used to it. What's the harm?

Your friends come around to visit every now and again, and you don't want them to be annoyed by the fire alarm, so you play loud music and take them to the living room, where they're far away from that pesky sound. There's no point in upsetting them. One of them points out that she can smell smoke, and you hilariously deflect by telling her that she's probably just having a stroke.

One day you decide to get a fireman (therapist) to come around to check. JUST IN CASE! It's probably nothing. You give the fireman a tour of the entire house, making small talk, "Yeah, I changed the batteries in the alarm, I opened some windows, occasionally I can smell a bit of smoke, but it's manageable. Just no idea where it's coming from. This room is my school years. This room is my relationship with my grandparents." Then the fireman points to a door that has smoke tendrils billowing out of the bottom of it and the handle is molten red. He suggests that maybe the fire is coming from there. You laugh him off. Silly fireman, no. That's just a regular room with a specific childhood memory in it. The smoke is definitely coming from the kitchen.

He comes with you to the kitchen, lets you explain all the appliances and the paint job you chose for the place. He walks with you around the rest of the house while you both try to find out where the fire is coming from, until eventually you think, *Maybe we should have a look in that room!* You open the door, and, sure enough, there's a massive blaze. You and the fireman try your best to put it out, and he teaches you how to notice whenever that fire starts going again. (There're going to be a lot of "fire" analogies from here on in, and if you're wondering why, turn on the news. Or go to California.)

I'm aware that therapy has become my "being vegan." Whenever my friends talk about what a hard time they've had or how difficult it was during lockdown, I'm always like, "Have you tried therapy? Oh. Em. Gee. You simply must. I've been doing it for nine months now, and I've let go of so much baggage. Honestly, just try it for a month, and see what happens!" because I now think everyone needs therapy. No exceptions. I think therapy should be compulsory, free, and universal.

It breaks my big soppy bleeding liberal heart that I get the benefit of therapy because I'm in a position where I can afford it and others can't. There are people who have much more difficult jobs who absolutely need therapy to deal with the shit they have to confront on a day-to-day basis. We expect men and women to perform surgery on babies, carry burned bodies out of buildings, go to a foreign country at the age of eighteen to shoot other eighteen-year-olds, dig mines, care for the dying, work sixteen-hour days for minimum wage—ALL OF THIS SHIT AND MORE. The fact that at the end of it we're like, "Just say, 'Hoo boy, rough day,' and move on like the rest of us, please," is insane and feels profoundly American.

Who had a good year in 2020? No one. It was a fucking nightmare. If you had a great 2020, please donate your body to science as it'll help us understand more about the chemical composition of the brains of sociopaths. If you didn't murder anyone in 2020, you nailed 2020. That's the only stipulation. "I'm an alcoholic now!" You nailed 2020. "I haven't seen my friends or family in months, and I've doubled in size." Wow. You fucking nailed 2020. "I buried her next to the kids." So close.

I remember at the start of the pandemic thinking, *Maybe this is the thing that will unite us as a species. A common enemy. Something we can all agree on and fight together. Something that is so big and terrifying it forces us to . . . Wait, what do you mean people are refusing to wear masks?* Yeah, I know, that optimism is my own fault. I should have known better than to have put any faith in one of the most gleefully, willfully misinformed nations that the world has ever seen.

It was a very difficult year for everyone. A global pandemic combined with economic collapse during a time of terrifying political polarization and multiple governments gaslighting their citizens, while we all desperately doom scroll the Internet trying to find a happy picture of a cat through all the lies, shouting, fearmongering, and mind-boggling stupidity is something that nobody should have to pretend was easy. Regardless of what side of the political spectrum you fall on, it's been a shitemare.

It can be hard to take your own emotions seriously. Do I have anxiety? Is this anxiety? It feels like anxiety. Surely, someone who doesn't have anxiety doesn't think about it all day long, but also surely the one stipulation for having anxiety can't be "being aware of anxiety." I was sad for a bit yesterday—is that depression or was I just sad? Am I depressed or is the world just depressing? Is this the correct amount of lack of hope to have at this point in time or is this a chemical imbalance in my noggin?

I think the fact of the matter is that we all have mental health problems. It's not a black-and-white issue, as I thought for so long. It's not as if there are some people who have mental health problems and those who don't. To think that there is a type of person, especially yourself, who is somehow immune to the struggles and crushing reality of the world we currently live in is arrogant to a point where I simply must applaud you in order to cover up my utter envy of having what I used to have.

It's like those cunts who have never done drugs and are doing them the first time. They take one ant's lungful of weed, let it sit in their mouths for five seconds, exhale, and go "I'm not feeling anything! Maybe I'm immune." Aye, Paul. You're the one person in the world who drugs don't affect. You're a medical marvel, and I've got Snoop Dogg on the phone here telling me to tell you that you're the real G.

Some people are scared of fire. Some people aren't. Some people are pyromaniacs. Some people become firemen. But nobody is *immune* to fire. A person that emphatically says, "You know what? I've actually never had a problem with fire. I lost my friend in a house fire and my mum burned her hand on a barbecue when she was younger, but I've never worried about ovens or any of that shit!" and then walks into a burning building, will not only be dead, but you'll think *I can't believe that fucking moron thought fire didn't affect him.*

I am that fucking moron. Or I was.

Some of you haven't been close enough to a fire to realize how much it burns. You will. The world is currently on fire. Trust me, you'll feel the heat real soon. I wish you all the best in it. Take steps, not to avoid the fire or to run away from it but to stop the burning or, at the very least, to deal with the burns afterward.

Therapy is one way, talking to friends is another, exercise is annoyingly useful. I fucking hate exercise. I hate it. I hate it. I HATE it. I do it because it's necessary, but I hate every goddamn fucking second of it and I want you to know that. I'm so bored with these social media "experts" harping on, "You know what? You do hate the first couple of months, but then you start to love the burn. You live for it. It becomes a habit." I'm here to tell you that's a fucking lie. Exercise is hell.

I have been in good shape since I was twenty-one. I got a personal trainer because I was a single narcissist who couldn't get laid off the back of his own personality, so I needed *something*. Since then, apart from the occasional sabbatical where I travel the world getting fucked up, I have worked out regularly. It has always sucked. I have never once enjoyed a fucking second of a gym session, a run, a jog. I still hate every fucking bit of it because working out sucks harder than Mike Pence's lips when he dreams about Mummy-Wummy taking off her Church cardigan.

Meditation is another way. I always used to hate meditation because The Pretentious Assholes got it first and absolutely drenched it in their own regurgitated cum. Those wanks, facing the sun and realigning their chakras on their dad's veranda going, "Yeah, no, it just works for me. The sun's energy lights up my insides, and it clears my mind of all thoughts." So do basic economic principles, you thick* cunt. How about you and Gwyneth Paltrow climb to the highest peak and shove coffee beans up your arse until something of worth leaves your mouth for the first time. I know that doesn't make it sound like I meditate. But I do. That's the scary part. This is me being peaceful and zen. Being so pure of thought and present in the current moment that I can directly mine the hate that exists in my heart and smelt it into solid gold slander.

This is another chapter where I don't think there is going to be a satisfying ending. I don't think there can be a happy ending to mental health, which is perhaps a sign that my therapy isn't going as well as I boldly claim. There can certainly be a sad one. À la Robin Williams. But a happy ending might not exist because you shouldn't think of there being a final point. You can't aim toward being a final product because you might live beyond that. It's all a process.

I often thought that having the person I wanted to become in my head was a good thing. I'd use it to inspire myself every day to become better. Instead, my brain decided to use it as a comparison point for everything I wasn't. You could be good at singing, but you're not. You could be good at baking muffins, but you're not. You could be good at self-love, but you're not, you big dumb poo-poo

---

* *Thick* in Scotland means stupid. As opposed to in America, where *thick* means big-bottomed. Which comes as a horrifying surprise to many American audiences when I describe my three-year-old goddaughter as "thick as pig shit."

head. I think I may need to find the balance between bullying myself and convincing myself that I'm the world's first International Treasure.

I should just lower my standards for happiness. It works. Instead of beating myself up for not knowing enough about American history, I can congratulate myself for having an interest in history and get a book on the subject. Instead of punishing myself for drinking too much over the weekend by going to the gym, I can reward myself for being a good host with strong weed and shitty TV. Instead of getting hung up on the fact that I haven't had a salad in my entire life, I think I'll celebrate the fact that my girlfriend clearly loves me for my personality, even though I devour ice cream and sweets.

It fills me with immense happiness just picturing my therapist reading that last paragraph and going, "What?! No! That's not what I said to do! At all! He's missed the entire point of the whole fucking thing! OH GOD, HOW MANY COPIES DID THIS SELL?!! HOW MANY LIVES WILL THIS SHIT ADVICE COST?! ARE THERE NO ETHICS IN PUBLISHING ANYMORE?" No, babe. Sorry. See you Monday.

My point is that life is long, and parts of it can be immensely shitty. You shouldn't focus on the future because you've got little control over it. All you can do is make sure the steps you take now are going in the direction of the future you want and be prepared for trips and falls along the way. Why focus on the past when you cannot change it? Mistakes will always linger there, and all you can do is learn from them and use them as benchmarks for how much you've improved since then. Focus on the now. The here and now. This one moment is all there is. Life is a series of infinite Nows.

And you're spending it reading this book. God, you really are a fucking loser.

Chapter 10

Love—and Cheaper, Funner Drugs

I've been told by my editor to write a chapter on love. His logic: We'll put it at the end, after all the "Religion is for dumb cunts" and "My ex-girlfriend made me want to kill myself" stuff, as a nice little palate cleanser. Just a way of convincing you, the reader (obviously an idiot), that this is a positive book. In the same way that you do a nice big smile and laugh whenever a child falls over so the little fucking moron doesn't realize how badly it is hurt.

I pushed back a bit at first. I didn't want to write a chapter on love. It's just a bit yucky. You don't want to hear about how in love I am in the same way I definitely don't want to hear how happy you are with whatever subpar consort with whom you decided to attempt to spend the remaining years of your life.

In this way, love is a lot like taking a shit. We all do it, and we all find our own shits fascinating, but we don't want to hear about one another's or see them on Instagram.

I hate seeing other people in love. There's just something

inherently awful about it. The way we swoon over each other. How one person walking into a room can suddenly change your whole mood. How some of us would literally die for our partner. It's utterly illogical. You come to rely on this person, need this person, and are sometimes less of yourself when they're not around, and that is, quite frankly, pathetic.

Feels fucking good, though.

I think that's why most of us hate seeing other people in love. It's a reflection of ourselves. Whenever you see friends pining over other people, laughing at their unfunny jokes and getting that cow-eyed look in their eyes when they see their partner, we are looking in a mirror and thinking, *Oh, fuck. Is that what I'm like when I love someone?* No. You're way worse.

I don't want you to know how pathetic I am now around my girlfriend. It's humiliating. Only she's allowed to know that. I have a persona to keep up. I'm the pseudo-intellectual narcissist, "anti-love" comedian who broke up all those couples and hates everything in the world. Not the little gimp boy who does a baby voice whenever his little Piggy is feeling an ickle bit iffy in her tum-tum. Fucking kill me dead.

I'd rather describe my shit to you. Fuck it. It's my book—I will. This morning I had what I like to call a "Hobbit shit." That doesn't mean it was small, hairy, and played by a British actor, but more that it could have come out in one whole piece but unnecessarily came out in three separate parts over a long period of time.

Ba dum dum tsh.

Another reason I didn't want to write a chapter on love is because I didn't think I'd be very good at writing about it. Some of the greatest artists of all time have tried and failed to convey what love is. And all poets. But that's because poetry isn't real art and anyone who says it is has tried to write it and failed.

I realize I've shat on poetry more than once and should explain my utter, utter disdain for the drivel.

Poetry is made by people who don't have enough talent to learn how to play an instrument, don't have the patience or skill to write a book, and can't carry a tune in a bucket. "Aww, look at me, I made my feelings rhyme."

Poetry fans' only argument for their shitty, shitty, shitty art form is that "Art is subjective." It's the shield they hide behind all the time whenever you calmly and rationally explain to them that the thing they love and hold dear is a stupid thing for little dumb idiots. Art is absolutely subjective, but it still takes skill. That dude who painted the *Mona Lisa*? Talented as fuck. Practiced loads of painting. Got really good at it. Painted a whole bunch of shit over the years. Even if you don't enjoy what he painted, you can't deny that the man was talented.

Michelangelo chiseled that big David guy. Very talented. Do you honestly think that was the first dick he'd ever chiseled? Not a chance. It took practice. Hours of it. He probably had an entire basement filled with semi-finished semis. Stubbing his toe on marble chodes all day long. His art took skill and sacrifice.

Ballet is a form of art whose beauty I don't even come close to understanding. Even though it doesn't speak to me in any way, shape, or form, I can still see the skill, practice, and talent that go into doing it. Same with opera. Same with musicals. Same with some modern art, too. I may not understand why welding forty thousand spoons together into the shape of a butterfly and calling it *Mother* is profoundly beautiful to vegan men named Sebastien, but I can still see the skill and talent that went into its craft. I might not feel the things these art forms are meant to make me feel, but to deny they are art is categorically false.

Most poems don't even fucking rhyme. The audacity! Even rap (also an art form) rhymes. "Poetry doesn't have to rhyme!" Yes. It fucking. Does. That's the only bit that makes it interesting. Otherwise it's just a sentence. Just a short sentence that you wrote over six stanzas to fabricate depth to your tedious ensemble of a personality. Just admit that you're sad and don't have the capability to express your sadness. That's fine. Not everyone should be an artist. I'd love to be a footballer, but I'm shit at football. I don't go around changing the rules of sports so my lazy ass can be considered an athlete.

Sometimes when I do stand-up there are parts of the show that aren't particularly funny. There are some serious elements over the course of my shows when the audience isn't laughing. But if I were to proudly walk around saying, "Comedy doesn't have to be funny," you would rightfully think that I was just a shit comedian who refused to admit that he'd chosen the wrong art form to pursue.

I'm stalling because I'm really trying to put this chapter off. It's very "off-brand" for me. My fans would be devastated if they knew how much I loved my girlfriend. Some of them think I'm an achievable celebrity fuck. And most of them would be right. I am one. Or was, until this annoying tart turned up and made me love her.

Piggy is the best thing that ever happened to me. I call her Piggy for several reasons, mainly that she has an intelligence level of close to that of a dog. I'm kidding. It's because her pussy tastes like bacon. Still kidding. I'm not going to name her in this book because I agreed to scrutiny when I stepped into the public eye. She has not done so. Should she wish to, she may. But that's her decision to make. Not mine.

For years and years and years I looked at people in love and it didn't make sense to me. I thought they were all pretending to be in love. Most of them are, still. There are people out there who are genuinely in love, but the shit they say feels rehearsed. It sounds fake. It's the cliché feeling of the catchphrases of love.

"My partner is my best friend." HAHAHAHA. You fucking loser. How do the rest of your friends feel about that? I bet you haven't told them because they'd be pissed off. What kind of loser is best friends with his girlfriend? Kai is my best friend. Jean is my best friend. Or Ally. Or the other Ali. Or any of the GOATs. Not my girlfriend. Idiots.

Well . . . ummm . . . My girlfriend *is* my best friend, man. She's just like Kai except she lets me do coke off her tits. Not to do a disservice to any of my longtime friends: I love you all dearly. But this woman brought her A game. When was the last time any of you sucked my dick, huh? Yeah. I thought so. Enjoy second place, where you rightfully belong.

There are people you want to fuck and there are people you want to hang around with. Very rarely do those things cross over. I never thought they would. Or could.

I have fucked plenty of people I would never want to hang out with. They are great company within the confines of a bedroom, but we have nothing in common except that we both think I'm great. I couldn't get most of those people out of my bed fast enough the second they started telling me about their day. They're the social equivalent of getting to a Davos chapter in a *Game of Thrones* book.

I couldn't fathom the person I wanted to fuck the most being the person I also wanted to hang around with the most. But I can tell my girlfriend anything. I confide in her about my deepest insecurities and she listens. Really listens. She listens because she loves me and not because she intends to use those insecurities against me later as a form of manipulation like one person I dated who turned out to be the single worst person I've ever met in my life.

In actual, real life, love is as lame as everyone makes it look and I couldn't be happier. I'm pathetic when I'm around this woman. I'm not even angry about it. I'd love to write a scathing chapter about how this selfish bitch waltzed into my life and made me fall in love with her. How I've had to change my life because life itself is unfathomable without her. It's worth anything to keep this person in my life. Compromise doesn't seem so bad when it's with someone so brilliant and perfect. Et cetera, et cetera. Wanky poetry shite.*

I can't. I've turned into everything I've hated and I'm loving it.

I'm not going to talk about that, though. None of you care. It's not what you want to read. I'd rather turn it around and give you a different message, and that message is this—I am still 100 percent correct about everything I said in *Jigsaw* and in this book's earlier chapters. I am a genius. Nay, a god. Neigh, a horse.

I wouldn't be happy in this relationship if I hadn't spent all those years single. I wouldn't know I was with the right person had I not spent all those years being alone, being selfish, and taking the time to work out what I wanted and how much I was willing to give up to get it—nothing.

It was worth the wait. It was worth those nights thinking, *Maybe it won't happen to me. Maybe I'm unlovable.*

---

* My editor keeps making me take the "e" off of "shite" because he thinks it's a spelling mistake. It isn't. It's a Scottish way of saying "shit," but it rhymes with height. Try saying it out loud. It's a joy.

Maybe I've numbed myself to intimacy. Maybe I'm broken. Maybe I'm gay. I do fancy the ever-loving fuck out of Mike Colter. (Google him. Sploosh.) I had almost resigned myself to being single forever and shagging whoever I wanted. That still sounds pretty good. If it doesn't work out with my girlfriend, I'll be sad, but at least I'll know threesomes are back on the table, and those are always fun.

I don't want people to watch *Jigsaw* and then come and read this and think, *That motherfucker, how dare he? He lied to us.* Maybe. We don't know yet. If this wench and I don't end up working out, then I'm the same dumbass I was before, and still technically right. I just temporarily forgot my own words. Didn't take my own advice, and if it bites me in the ass, prepare for *2 Jigsaw 2 Furious.* Win-win for everyone except my poor broken heart (which I'll then cash in. Don't worry about me).

I spent seven years as a single adult. Seven years not knowing if I'd ever get the opportunity to be a dad. It's not a long time. Many have spent more time single, and to those people I say—keep going. Learn to love being single and being alone. It can be tough, but it can also be brilliant. It's down to you to make it work. If you don't love yourself, you're going to spend the rest of your life auditioning people to do it for you. We all know how crazy it is to leave your emotions in someone else's hands.

If you love yourself and enjoy being single, then you can't be threatened with a breakup. You can still be broken up with, but it means that if there's an argument or an ongoing problem with your partner, he or she can't force you to change a part of who you are (at least a part you don't want to change), because when the words "You can't have me anymore" are said, the meaning is now "You can have anyone else," and that's not a threat, that's a buffet.

I don't want to get too much into self-love. I don't want to be one of those head-mic-wearing, positive-attitude, "The universe will make it happen if you believe" con artists who should all be kicked in the shins to death. The other day I found a Facebook page where they had taken one of my rants from *Jigsaw,* but they left out the punch line. They just left in the setup to the joke because it was positive without the gut-punch "fuck you" punch line at the end and I'm furious. It's a fucking meme of me telling everyone to love themselves. Gross. I've never felt so misrepresented in my life. I should sue. Whoever did that shouldn't love themselves but go and fuck themselves.

At the same time, though, I am fortunate enough to be one of only seven comedians in the whole wide world who doesn't have depression. Many of my friends have it and it sucks. Some of the greatest people in the world have an enemy living behind their eyes—their brain. I find it easy to love myself and I'm a pile of shit. There are brilliant people out there who don't love themselves as much as I do, and that's unfair. We all should love ourselves. Well, not all of us. There are some people I think could do with a healthy little bit of depression just to give them some perspective.

I'm also still in the "honeymoon" phase of my relationship as of this writing. We're massively in love. We don't fight. We don't argue. We don't even annoy each other. This will 100 percent last forever and you can't convince me otherwise.

Other adults in longer, more successful relationships will be reading this and laughing. Looking forward to the next book, which will inevitably be titled *Fuck You, I Don't Want to Talk About It.* Maybe it will get to the point where we wind each other up and grate on each other. Where we do have to compromise in order to save the relationship.

Or maybe . . . just maybe . . . I've hit the jackpot and you are still in the wrong fucking relationship.

What if all that compromise stuff isn't true? I've been with this woman for three years now and we have never had an argument. Our relationship is incredibly healthy. Every day I fall more in love with her. Maybe I've found true love and you haven't. All that compromise and effort and work that you insist I need to prepare for is something you have learned to put up with in order to stay in the safe bubble of a relationship that you have become so used to.

Maybe you haven't found "the One." Maybe you just found . . . one.

How do I know my girlfriend is "the One"? I don't, but I have my suspicions. We were on holiday recently and all the other couples around us wanted to go on a hike up a mountain to get a view of the island. I didn't want to do this because I enjoy fun and if I wanted to see a good view of the island I was on, I would Google it. And I did, in fact. From the bottom of the mountain. I saw aerial shots, side shots, panoramic views. More beautiful angles than were physically capable of being seen from the top of the mountain, and at the expense of my 4G instead of my legs.

Relationships are about compromise and you have to work to make them work, I'm told. So if my girlfriend wanted to climb up that mountain, then I would have done that because that's what relationships take. Work, work, work. That's why they're so fun. But when we got to the bottom of the mountain my girlfriend looked up and said, "Fuck that. Want to go drink?" I nearly proposed on the spot. The other couples went up the mountain. Sweating, panting, and trying their best not to moan in front of their partners so that they didn't have to say, "Whose fucking idea was this?" Me and my strumpet stayed at the bottom of the mountain, playing with every dog that passed by and Googling better views from different parts of the world.

Surprisingly, I haven't been able to get into trouble with my girlfriend. I haven't been trying, but I still fuck up. But here's the thing: When I fuck up she seems to understand that it was a mistake. When I explain my reasoning for my dumb decision and she understands that it came from a place of stupidity rather than malice, she does this really weird thing—she believes me and never holds it against me.

And I've done some shit that would have gotten me murdered in previous relationships. Here's a list of things off the top of my head that I think would get most people, including me in past relationships, into trouble with their partner:

- Once, I accidentally sat her at a table where the only four other members of the table were people I had had sex with in the past.
- I missed her birthday because I was on tour. (I sent presents, but I wasn't present.)
- I keep forgetting most things about her. The other day she asked me how many tattoos she had and it was only at that moment that I found out she even had tattoos. Two. I think.
- I call her these names: bitch, dumbass, ugly, slut, slag, cow, cunt, fuckhead, doll, sugar tits, wench, Piggy, pig slut, her sister's name, her mother's name, and toots, because I'm really into '80s office sexism.
- She was having a shower before work this morning and for no reason whatsoever, other than it was funny, I went in and threw freezing-cold water over her.
- I don't text her back all the time. Sometimes I forget. Sometimes I'm too high. Sometimes I can't be bothered. Sometimes we won't talk for days while I'm on tour.
- I killed both of her parents in front of her without blinking.
- All right, that one was a lie. But you get my point.

Now, some of you are looking at that list and thinking, *Those aren't bad, Daniel. None of that should get you into trouble. You're clearly harboring issues from previous relationships. None of that stuff would get me in trouble, either.* Congratulations. Not only are you correct, but you're also in a healthy relationship. I have merely arrived at the conclusion that you and your soul mate arrived at years ago when you fell in love. Well done, us.

Some of you, though . . . Some of you are reading that list and thinking, *That would get me into serious trouble. In fact, I've been in trouble for a lot less. I couldn't even* tell *my partner if I'd done something like that. I'd never hear the end of it. My partner scares me.* Uh-oh. Guess who's in the wrong relationship? Yes, you are.

God, if this book leads to more breakups, I don't think I'll ever stop writing or touring. Or talking. Or ejaculating at the thought of my own power.

What you're about to witness is called "hubris." A man confidently telling you he'll never have to compromise in his relationship that is only three years old in an attempt to convince you that compromising in a relationship of thirty years is bad.

But fuck it, let's drive this nail home, shall we?

If most of your relationship is you changing parts of yourself, hiding parts of your personality from your partner, and living in some form of fear of your partner's reaction to what you do, especially if it's unintentional, then congratulations, you have wasted most of your life.

That's not love. Really. It's not. I'm thirty years old. I think I know what I'm talking about. Over the years you have compromised and changed and altered yourself. Chipped away at parts of yourself. Small parts of yourself that in the moment you decided didn't matter. They weren't important in the long run. It was worth changing that part of yourself in order to make the other person happy, or, at the very least, shut the fuck up for just one goddamn second.

You chipped and you chipped and you chipped over the years, and now you are just a sad little rock on the ground with no shape, essence, or love about you. The pile of rubble that was your personality is now bigger and more impressive than you are as an entire human being. You changed who you are to become someone you are not for someone that you don't like all that much. You did this because when you entered your relationship you disliked yourself so much that instead of finding someone who loved you for who you are, you instead found someone who had one thing in common with you and that thing was that neither of you ever really loved you for you.

You gave up who you were for love and now you are no longer there. And you wonder why you are sad.

You'll both have your excuses for why you're staying together. You'll repeat them to yourselves as a mantra. In the hopes that saying it enough times will magically make it true.

It's for the kids. Despite the fact that your children do not want to live in a house with two people that do not like each other. That's not what they want to believe a relationship is, two people who can merely coexist. What sort of example is that to set for the people that you truly love? Look yourself in the eyes and ask yourself this question: Would you allow your children to settle for the type of relationship that you are in? No. You fucking wouldn't.

You'll tell yourself it's too late. You're past it. That time of your life is gone and it's not worth taking such a risk to go back onto the market. Stop seeing it as a fucking market, then. You are not cattle and you are not up for auction. Being single does not mean being for sale. Your value does not come from how much other people want to be with you but from how much you want to be with yourself. Would you rather spend the rest of your days being someone you're not in order to be surrounded by people you tolerate, dislike, or hate, or would you rather spend your life being happy with yourself and alone?

We have one fucking life on this planet. One go. One shot. We make mistakes and we fuck up constantly. But just because you've fallen into shit doesn't mean you have to wallow in it forever. Get back up and take a fucking shower.

Christ, I've gone self-love again. Damn it.

If that's what it takes for some of you to go out there and end your lackluster relationship, then so be it. I'll be that guy for a few more minutes.

I don't know who you are or what you do and I don't really care. My advice might be the worst thing in the entire world for you. It might fuck up your entire life. But I doubt it. Every person I've spoken to who broke up or got divorced because of *Jigsaw* says they are happier than they were before. I still get hundreds of emails every month thanking me for giving people the kick up the arse that it took to get them out of their relationship. One hundred percent positive feedback. But maybe that's because the dead can't write emails.

I think 95 percent of people on this earth deserve happiness. Five percent deserve absolute suffering. Sadly, it's never the people who should suffer that do. So let's just assume you fall into the 95 percent that deserve to be happy. Go do it! I can make you happy for a few hours a day with this book or my stand-up. Chocolate, sex, booze, drugs, cars, knitting, animals, and all sorts of other stuff can make you happy for longer periods of time. The only person that can keep you happy forever is yourself, and if you're finding that hard, it's probably because you are not surrounding yourself with the right people, and you should probably start with yourself.

Make yourself happy and then maybe you'll be lucky enough to find someone who makes you happier. If you don't, you're still happy.

Go and just fucking love yourself so I can stop being this self-love guru that I never wanted to be but now have to be because I have a savior complex and I love the attention.

Despite the fact that I am besotted by my girlfriend, I do not think she is "the One." I don't believe in "the One." If I wasn't around, I'm sure she'd find someone else who loved her as much as I do. I reckon she could find thousands.

Millions, if she lowered her expectations. Tens of millions, if they lowered theirs.

Same goes for me. As much as I want to spend the rest of my life with her, I might be wrong. I'm not arrogant enough to think that there is only one person out there good enough for me. I think a lot of people who believe in "the One" don't necessarily believe there is only one person out there for them. Rather, they believe themselves good enough for only one person. Sad, sad, sad.

Love is the greatest feeling in the world and the people who feel they don't deserve to be loved are the ones that weren't loved enough in the first place.

Cards on the table: I have no idea how to end this bad boy. I feel like there should be some profound closing statement that sums up the whole book, the way I was taught to do in English class. I don't have one. I think there's enough profound stuff already, if you're willing to wade through the shit that surrounds it.

Maybe I could be ironic and end with a poem about love, but alas, I cannot lower myself like that. I am too talented for poetry.

The reason I can't end this book properly is because there are no actual answers to any of this. These pages are all just my thoughts on life and love that some people seem to enjoy hearing. Maybe some of you didn't. That's fair. Just as long as you remember that I still have your money and I'm going to spend it on drugs and other things you don't like just to spite you.

I can't summarize love. I can't summarize relationships. I pretend I have the answers to all of the questions because I like playing the part of the person who knows everything. It's a lot more fun than the truth—that I know as much about love as everyone else.

And that is very little.

So, in conclusion, this book has been a waste of both of our times. Thank you.

Acknowledgments

I fucking hate acknowledgment chapters. I never read them. "I'd like to take this time to thank"—just fucking phone them then, you twat. Why don't you personally thank those people face-to-face? Instead of making me trawl through another three pages listening to you wank off your high school bully because he taught you about struggling or some shit just so you can bring your word count up to something acceptable.

All that aside, having now written a book and realizing I was probably the least important person involved in the whole process, allow me sincerely and wholeheartedly to thank:

Jess Purcell, my Knopf publicist—a woman whose job it is to convince people that I'm not as much of a cunt as I clearly am. Thanks for lying to people on my behalf, Jess. You are a diamond.

Michael O'Brien, my U.S. publicist and another master of making me come across as a decent human being. Thank you for always being a friend in New York. I enjoy our little adventures, and I'm sorry for all the ranting I make you put up with.

Sara Eagle, my social media/marketing guru at Knopf— I hate social media almost as much as I hate my fans, and Sara managed to keep me murder free during this whole process. Patience of a saint. I don't pay her nearly enough.

John Gall—you like the jacket of this book? Of course you do. Stupid question. John did that. John did that midcoronavirus, too. While everyone was screaming, "Are you sure we should put two corpses fucking on the cover of a book being released mid-plague?," John stood his ground admirably and for that I commend him.

The rest of the Knopf team—Paul Bogaards, Chris Gillespie, and Reagan Arthur—thank you for doing whatever it is you actually do. I'm sure you told me at some point, but I was too busy enjoying the free coffee in your offices while I laughed internally at the absolute stupidity you have shown by giving me my own book. And you were really encouraging and supportive about it, too. You backed me from the start. You absolute fucking morons. Thank you so much.

Peter Gethers—the man who not only asked me to write this book, but the man who allowed me to keep in all those rimming references. Touché, Mr. Gethers, touché. Thank you sincerely for this incredible opportunity, your constant encouragement, praise, and whisky sessions. I never considered this as something I would be capable of, and I wouldn't have been if not for you. I owe you a Roseburn.

My manager Marlene—without you I wouldn't have my career, my house, my car, my specials, my ego, or my mental health problems. I wouldn't be the man or comedian I am today if not for you—take that as a compliment if you wish. Thanks for always being there. Sorry I'm a whiny cunt sometimes, but in my defense—you are incredibly annoying. Having said that, there is not a smarter, kinder, tougher, or more hardworking rep on the planet. Thank you for everything you've done for me. Sincerely. (Also, take a fucking day off, would you?)

Rachel Rusch—my incredibly sweet, kind, and supportive American agent. Thanks for taking a chance on me all of those long, long years ago. Your support has always meant the world to me.

Matt & Ari, Jorge & Tom—thanks for all your hard work on my behalf. I do deeply appreciate it, though I don't tell any of you nearly enough.

JP Buck—you unbelievably handsome bastard. Thanks for letting me do the abortion joke on national television. There's a bunch of other stuff I definitely owe you thanks for, like the career in America, but to be honest the abortion joke is the big one for me. Love you, bud.

Ian Coburn—thanks for the cold, hard reality checks you give me. I may not have appreciated them at the time, but in hindsight they were exactly what I needed. You were right. Never send me to Bradford again.

To the GOATs—thanks for the countless problems you've helped me with over the years, and thanks for the countless more problems you've given me. Love you boys.

My family—for not molesting or beating me, even when I deserved it. Thanks for your constant, sickening support. I'll put you all in a nice home one day.

Piggy—turns out they won't let you put a middle finger emoji in here, so just assume I'm doing it. 2019 and 2020 would have been a much bigger clusterfuck if not for you. Thank you for keeping me sane, grounded, and happier than I've ever been. I love you lots, you little fucking rat.

Kai—thanks for always having my back and being there for me. Especially in Hong Kong. Thanks also for being the first friend to read this book fully. Your comments were kind, thoughtful, and encouraging. Your spelling corrections were not only unnecessary, but wrong. They literally have an editor for that. Thanks, though.

Jean—you got an entire chapter, too; stop being greedy. Miss you, come home. Bonne nuit, Mark Latimer.

Mum & Dad—what have you done for me recently, huh? (Kidding, I love you and what not.)

Matthew & Jack—and you two, twats. (Love you, too.)

All my other friends—I know you didn't get a mention in the book, and you'll not find your name here either. Haha. Sorry. None of my readers know nor care who you are, and I'm not going to lie to them and pretend you helped. I did this. Love you, though. Thanks for the support.

God—thank you for walking with me through the hard times and carrying me through the really hard times. You are my savior, my lord, and my inspiration. Thank you for life and for every breath that I take. Your love flows through my veins. To spread your message of love is my purpose, and I thank you for giving me it. And thanks for the big cock, too. That was nice of you. Do me a favor and stop killing random disabled children for no fucking reason though, would ya?

A Note About the Author

The author finds About the Author sections wanky and outdated. He would just like you to watch his fucking comedy specials. The publisher, on the other hand, would like you to know that Daniel Sloss is an internationally acclaimed, award-winning Scottish comedian and writer who has released three groundbreaking comedy specials. He has created and toured eleven solo shows across fifty countries to rave reviews and has, to date, sold out six extended sessions Off-Broadway in New York. In addition, for more than a decade Daniel has been one of the biggest ticket sellers at the world's biggest arts festival, the Edinburgh Festival Fringe. The 2018–2019 global tour of *Daniel Sloss: X* spanned 300 performances, including at the London Palladium, and with the Moscow Arena date becoming Russia's biggest-ever English-language comedy show. *X* premiered on HBO in the USA and Canada in November 2019 and has rolled out across the world, including a UK theatrical release. Netflix is streaming "Daniel Sloss Live Shows: *Dark* and *Jigsaw*" in 190 countries and twenty-six languages. *Jigsaw* has infamously caused more than 120,000 breakups and has been cited in more than 300 divorces. Fans even bring their divorce decrees for him to autograph at shows. And yet Daniel still believes in love. Daniel is thirty and lives in Scotland, his "forever home."

A Note on the Type

This book was set in Adobe Garamond. Designed for the Adobe Corporation by Robert Slimbach, the fonts are based on types first cut by Claude Garamond (ca. 1480–1561). Garamond was a pupil of Geoffroy Tory and is believed to have followed the Venetian models, although he introduced a number of important differences, and it is to him that we owe the letter we now know as "old style." He gave to his letters a certain elegance and feeling of movement that won their creator an immediate reputation and the patronage of Francis I of France.

Typeset by Scribe,
Philadelphia, Pennsylvania

Printed and bound by Berryville Graphics,
Berryville, Virginia

Designed by Michael Collica